Fly Fishing Georgia's Toccoa River

Your complete guide to fly fishing for trout on north Georgia's Toccoa River, including the Upper Toccoa, the Delayed Harvest Section, and the Toccoa Tailwater.

By Steve Hudson

Fly Fishing Georgia's Toccoa River

Your complete guide to fly fishing for trout on northern Georgia's Toccoa River, including the Upper Toccoa, the Delayed Harvest section, and the Toccoa Tailwater.

By Steve Hudson

Published by
Chattahoochee Media Group LLC
121 Wills Lane
Alpharetta, GA 30009
(770) 329-7642

www.chattahoocheemedia.com
Like us on Facebook at **www.facebook.com/chattahoocheemedia**

ISBN 978-1-941600-08-5

Copyright © 2015 by Steve Hudson

All rights reserved. No part of this publication may be reproduced, stored in a retrieval system, or transmitted in any form or by any means – electronic, mechanical, photocopy, recording, or any other – except for brief quotations in reviews, without the prior written permission of the publisher.

Manufactured in the United States

> Outdoor recreation is an inherently risky activity. Neither the author nor Chattahoochee Media Group assume any responsibility or liability for any losses, accidents or injuries of any sort sustained by anyone who engages in the activities described in this book or who visits the locations described in this book.

> # For John Marsh,
> ### who first showed me the Toccoa River

Acknowledgements

No book happens in a vacuum, and that's especially true for this one. Many folks have contributed to its creation.

I'd like to thank David Hulsey, who has guided on the Toccoa (along with his wife Becky, also a Toccoa guide) for many years. David freely shared his knowledge and insights and has been a great help from the very beginning of this project. David and Becky are both consummate fly fishers and patient teachers, and it's been a privilege to share the water with them.

I'd also like to say thank you...

...to Jake Darling and Jimmy Harris of Unicoi Outfitters, who generously shared their knowledge (and some great photos).

...to James Bradley of Reel 'em In Guide Service for sharing additional insights and some fine photos too.

...to Jeff Turner of Blue Ridge Fly Fishing, who shared many tips on fishing this great river.

...to Amanda Hoppers and John Alford for coming along on all those trips to the Toccoa as this book was coming together.

...to the Georgia Department of Natural Resources for working so hard to provide such great fishing opportunities for Georgia anglers.

...to my bride Ann for letting me go fishing even when I should be cutting the grass.

...and to God, for everything.

Contents

Preface
6   Turn left...to the Toccoa!

Meet the Toccoa
8   Getting to know a river
9   How it got its name
9   Growth of the fishery
10   What's the best time of year to visit?

Getting ready
14   Tackle selection
16   Gear for wading
16   Gear for floating
18   Choosing the right flies for your Toccoa adventure
20   Month-by-month Toccoa "bug chart"

Upper Toccoa (Deep Hole to Sandy Bottom)

30   Upper Toccoa overview
30   "Can I fish here?"
31   What's what and where's where
32   Getting help from maps
33   Floating the upper Toccoa
35   Upper Toccoa without a boat
37   Upper Toccoa fly fishing strategies

Delayed Harvest
40   What is Delayed Harvest?
42   Toccoa DH overview
42   Accessing the DH
44   Wade or float?
48   DH fly choice
49   DH strategies

The tailwater

52 How we got it
53 Wade or float?
54 Tailwater map
56 Figuring out releases
61 Fishability at different flows
67 Tailwater safety
70 Tips for tailwater first-timers
71 Section 1: Dam to Tammen Park
75 Section 2: Tammen Park to Curtis Switch
79 Section 3: Curtis Switch to Horseshoe Bend Park
83 Section 4: Horseshoe Bend Park to Toccoa River Park

A Toccoa River gallery
86 Scenes from the Toccoa.

Appendix
88 Area fly shops and guide services...and license info.

PREFACE

Turn left...to the Toccoa

Even though I've fished northern Georgia for – well, let's just say for a while now, I always tend to go to the same general areas. For a long time, it seemed that whenever the fishing urge would strike, I would always head to the same patch of mountains and fish the same old set of streams.

Like a lot of fly fishers, I'm a creature of habit.

Sometimes habits can be good. But other times they just keep you from finding new things...or new water.

That's where my mind was one day several years ago when the phone rang right before supper. It was my friend John Marsh, an outdoorsman and a gentleman if ever there was one.

John and I talked for a few minutes.

Then he asked a question.

"So how about it?" he asked. "Want to try some new water?"

New water?

Hmmm. Believe it or not, good ol' habit-bound me had actually been entertaining that very concept. I'd been thinking that fishing had gotten into a bit of a rut, and maybe new water would put freshness and adventure back into the mix. *Like trying something new from an old, familiar menu,* I told myself. *It might be fun.*

And so I said, "Sure!"

As it turned out, the new water that John had in mind was the Toccoa River. I don't really know why I'd never fished it before... perhaps because my trusty old red truck always turned right instead of left at the U.S. 76 intersection.

But that was about to change, because tomorrow I'd try something new and make a left turn toward the Toccoa!

And so "tomorrow" came. I made the left turn, and I discovered a new adventure in Georgia trout fishing that I enjoy to this day.

In the years since, the Toccoa has become one of my favorite fishing destinations. Many other anglers share that opinion, too, and it's easy to see why: miles of river, spectacular scenery, nice wading, great driftboat runs, lots of hatches – and lots of fish.

Although the Toccoa is on its way to becoming one of those "destination" waters, there's never been a complete guide to the many fishing opportunities it offers – until now.

I hope that this book will get you excited about checking out this river. So make that left turn. I think you'll be glad you did.

Tight lines, and see you on the Toccoa!

Steve Hudson

Part 1:

Meet the Toccoa

A quick introduction to a great Georgia river

Photo courtesy Unicoi Outfitters

Meet the Toccoa

An introduction to a river that may change the way you view southern trout fishing.

First, a question: How do you define a friend?

There's been a lot written about that over the years. Most agree that a friend is (among other things) patient with you, kind to you, gives you second chances, and generally makes your life better.

By that definition, and if you'll allow me to get just a little anthropomorphic, I suppose a river could be called a "friend."

If that's the case, then let me introduce you to a friend of mine...

My friend is north Georgia's Toccoa River. A year-round trout stream located in north-central Georgia within easy driving distance of Atlanta, it originates in Union County and flows roughly south-to-north through Fannin County on its way to McCaysville, Ga., and Tennessee. At the state line, it becomes the Ocoee (of Olympics fame).

Within Georgia, the Toccoa has a length of not quite 60 miles. The uppermost headwaters are mostly on private land, so they're pretty much off the table as far as fishing is concerned. However, starting at a place called Deep Hole, you begin to find public access to fishable water.

I've gotten to know the Toccoa River over the years, and I have learned that it does indeed meet the requirements of our "friend" definition. To wit: It's been very patient with me as I've learned its ways, giving me all the second chances I've needed...it's been kind to me, often better than I deserve...and it very mercifully has not once reminded me of botched casts, missed fish, and other such missteps along the way. I could go on, but you get the idea.

How the Toccoa got its name

How did the Toccoa get its name?

One undeniably appealing story is that the name comes from the Cherokee term for "beautiful." Certainly, this is a spectacularly beautiful river. The scenery along much of the Toccoa is incredible, and you inevitably seem to end up felling like you're exploring wilderness a thousand miles from everything. You could easily see how this river might earn a name that means "beautiful."

But a more probable explanation is that the word Toccoa evolved from another Cherokee term, *Ta-gwa-hi*, which means "place where the Catawba lived."

Here's how that might have led to the river's name. The Cherokee and Catawba apparently did not get along, possibly because Catawba raiding parties kept trying to set up settlements in Cherokee territory. The Cherokee apparently responded forcefully to these incursions, and it appears that some of the places where the Catawba were encountered subsequently came to be referred to as *Ta-gwa-hi*.

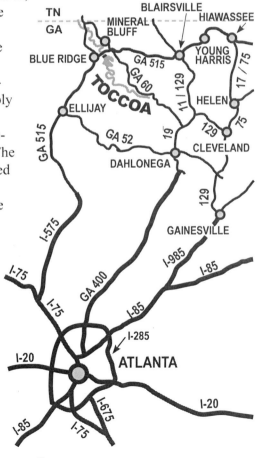

Growth of the fishery

Regardless of how it came by its name, there's no doubt that the Toccoa today offers some great fishing. Yet for many years the river and its fly fishing potential coasted along under the radar, despite the fact that

it's not too far from the big city of Atlanta. That may have been because of its out-of-the-way and, at the time, somewhat hard-to-get-to location. At least that was how we saw it in my house, where I recall hearing as a child how difficult it was to get up into that part of the state. "Those roads are too twisty," the grown-ups would always say.

There was also the matter of water releases from Blue Ridge Dam. For a long time the perception was that releases from that dam were unpredictable – especially important since those releases directly affected the tailwater portion of the Toccoa.

Finally, there was the matter of access. A lot of the Toccoa flows through private property, and landowners along the river

What's the best time of year on the Toccoa?

Trying to decide when to visit the Toccoa River? Good news – it's a river that can offer good fishing all year long.

David Hulsey, who has guided and fished on the Toccoa for many years, has great insight into what this river is like at different times of year. As he notes, the "best" time to fish the Toccoa may depend on what you consider to be the "best" fishing. Certain seasons consistently bring certain types of fishing, and the knowledgeable Toccoa fly fisher will key in on his or her favorites.

Say your plans call for a late February and early March trip. That's good timing, for that's when the Toccoa's well-known black caddis hatches appear.

"That hatch lasts about three weeks," David says.

Interestingly enough, David adds, dry flies may not be the best way to fish these hatches. Instead, he suggests emerger patterns. That's because the adult black caddis are on the water for only a very short time, while the emergers are active just about continuously.

"Black soft hackles imitate emergers coming off the bottom of the river," he says. He adds that spent adults are available to fish for long periods of time, too, so imitations of spent black caddis also work.

If you'll be there during May and June, you'll be perfectly positioned to enjoy the Toccoa's fabled sulphur hatches.

What makes these hatches so great?

"It's the number of bugs, the consistency of the daily hatches, and the number of fish coming up to take them," David explains.

The sulphur hatches may start gradually. But as the hatches grow in size and as more bugs begin to appear, he adds, "the river's trout definitely get those sulphurs on their minds."

To imitate these bugs, David suggests sulphur comparaduns, yellow palmers or "any kind of sulphur emerger with CDC in it."

As spring gives way to summer, terrestrial activity picks up. Topwater fishing with various terrestrial imitations can be good all the way through September.

What if your plans call for a fall trip? Then you may want to bring a heavy rod and some big streamers to tempt the rivers spawning browns.

"That's a good time to catch a monster on the Toccoa," David says, but he adds that it takes big flies to do so. How big? "Articulated streamers up to 6 or 7 inches long can do the trick," he says.

Six or seven inches? That's a big fly! But the payoff may be a fish like his personal best, a brown in the 25-inch range.

If you find that the only time you can fish the Toccoa is winter, you'll still find good fishing. The river's fabled Delayed Harvest section offers great wintertime fishing; on the tailwater, you can go deep with big rubber-legged stonefly nymphs or go small with tiny nymphs or dries.

"For solitude, winter is a perfect time to fish the Toccoa," he says. "Often it's like having the river to yourself."

The good news is that the "best" time on this river is pretty much year-round. As David so aptly puts it, "You can always find fish on the Toccoa!"

have long been protective of their private property rights.
Then some things began to change.

One was the construction of Georgia Highway 515, a four-laner which arches through this part of Georgia to provide significantly improved access. In fact, 515 crosses the Toccoa near the upper end of the tailwater and within sight of Blue Ridge Dam. The water release situation improved, too, and even the matter of access began to ease a bit as landowners began to see that most of today's river users (including fly fishers) are stewards of the resource and are interested in protecting and preserving it. Hopefully that trend will continue.

The fish and the fishing

Today, the Toccoa River is a multi-faceted fly fishing destination that draws anglers from across the country. For that fishery, anglers owe a loud word of thanks to a strong support constituency which includes (among others) the Georgia Department of Natural Resources, U.S. Fish and Wildlife Service, Tennessee Valley Authority, and several Trout Unlimited chapters.

When did the river first become a significant trout fishery? The headwaters presumably held trout from the beginning. And the tailwater?

"The tailwater has been stocked every year since 1976," notes John Damer, a fisheries biologist with the Wildlife Resources Division of Georgia DNR. "But there were even a few stocking events that took place before that," he adds, noting that the earliest one he knows of was 8,000 rainbow trout stocked there in 1963.

Today, the Toccoa is widely recognized for the great recreational opportunities that it offers. These range from the Toccoa River Canoe Trail above Blue Ridge Lake, to the specially managed Delayed Harvest water which starts at the end of the canoe trail, to the world-class tailwater trout fishery which extends for close to 14 miles below Blue Ridge Dam. That's a lot of fishing, and much of it can be very, very good. In fact, Fannin County now bills itself as the "Trout Fishing Capital of Georgia."

That's a strong claim. Does it live up to the billing?

That you will have to decide for yourself.

But I'll tell you this. The Toccoa is now among my favorite Georgia trout fisheries – and since I've lived here in Georgia for most my life, I've got a lot of other waters to compare it to.

So settle in for an adventure that may change the way you look at southern trout fishing – an unforgettable fishing adventure on Georgia's Toccoa River.

Part 2:
Getting ready

What you'll need to fish the Toccoa

- Choosing the right tackle
- Wading gear
- Float tubes and boats
- Choosing the right flies

The right gear

What gear is right for the Toccoa? That's an important question that we'll look at here.

It's important to pick the right gear for a Toccoa outing, and what is "best" depends on how, where and when you're fishing.

Tackle options

When fly fishers ask about the "right" gear, they're usually asking about rod, reel, line and leaders.

Rod: What's the best rod for the Toccoa? That varies with location and season. For the popular Toccoa tailwater or the Delayed Harvest section, most opt for an 8.5- to 9-foot, 5- or 6-weight rod. Such a rod will handle longer distances, and for close-in fishing (such as nymphing) it offers advantages in terms of reach and line control. A 5- or 6-weight can handle most flies you're likely to use on the tailwater. However, if you'll be focusing on throwing bigger streamers or heavier nymph rigs, lean toward the 6-weight – or even something a little heavier.

Can you go lighter? A 4-weight is fine if you'll be using only lighter flies. However, a 4-weight won't handle heavy flies or heavy nymphing

Most Toccoa River trips start with assembling the needed gear – and many fly fishers find that gearing up for a trip is half the fun!

rigs (not to mention factors such as wind) as well as a 5- or 6-weight.

Toccoa fly fishers who are floating the river in a drift boat or raft often carry several rigged rods, each set up for a different kind of fishing.

Reel: Reel selection is straightforward. You want a reel that'll hold your fly line as well as backing, and on this river a good drag system can be a factor too (if you're lucky enough to tangle with one of the Toccoa giants). Either disk or click drags will do the job.

Line: First and foremost, the line should be sized to match your rod. As for taper, a weight-forward (WF) taper will work fine.

What about floating vs. intermediate or sink-tip? A floating line is fine for dry or nymph fishing and will often do the job with streamers, too. However, a sink-tip line (with a short leader) will help get your streamers down deeper while letting you use lighter-weight, more lifelike flies. If you plan to fish streamers exclusively, consider a sink-tip line.

Leaders: The Toccoa can be exceptionally clear, and these fish get a fair amount of pressure. They become smart fast! One way to tip the odds in your favor is use a leader that won't spook them. A good tapered nylon leader works fine, and fluorocarbon is great if the budget allows. Choose tippet size to match the flies you'll be using.

What about length? When fishing dries or nymphs, go with a leader in the 9-foot range. When fishing streamers with an intermediate or sink-tip line, you can use shorter (and heavier) leaders in the 4- to 6-foot range.

Tippet: Remember to carry a couple of spools of spare tippet – one to match the tippet size of your leader and one that's one size finer. For example, if you're using a leader with a 5X tippet, carry a spool of 5X tippet material plus a spool of 6X tippet.

You can use the finer material if you find you need to go with a finer tippet but don't want to change out the leader. You can also use it to attach droppers when fishing with multiple nymphs, and that may help you save flies when deep nymphing. Why? Because if the bottom fly hangs up on an underwater obstruction and you need to break it off, the finer material will probably break first. That may save your top fly.

Fly floatant: Don't forget a bottle of fly floatant on your Toccoa trip. Fast riffles will drench your dry flies, and a good floatant will help keep those flies floating high and dry.

Split shot: On the Toccoa, you'll find some very deep holes that beg for a deep-drifting nymph, and the way to go deep is to use enough split shot to get the fly down where you want it. In deep water, you'll need large split shot. Leave the smaller shot at home.

Strike indicators: You'll probably want to carry some strike indicators with you on your Toccoa adventures. Choose indicators that will float with the amount of weight you plan to use. Thingamabobbers float well and are easy to see, and a large yarn indicator will float well too if you treat it with floatant before it gets wet.

Gear for wading

Waders: Chest waders are the norm on the Toccoa. The varying depth in many areas makes hip boots impractical, for you'll almost certainly top them when trying to wade through deeper spots.

Can you wade wet (that is, without waders?). Certainly not during the winter, when the Toccoa is cold – "excrutiatingly cold" is the way one young angler described it one day last January! In fact, most fly fishers opt out of wet wading at any time of year, though a few hearty souls delight in telling of their wet-wading adventures in this ice-cold water. Me, I'd rather not be cold while fishing, so I use waders year-round. Breathable waders will keep you comfortable regardless of the season.

Wading staff: One item of wading gear that many Toccoa regulars consider essential is a wading staff. While Toccoa wading is "good" by many standards, you'll find plenty of areas with rocks, cobbles, ledges and dropoffs. A wading staff is a great help in those areas.

And here's one more thing to consider: On the tailwater, a wading staff could literally be a lifesaver if you should be caught in an unexpected release and must move fast to exit the river as quickly as possible.

Polarized glasses: The Toccoa can be remarkably clear, and polarized glasses will help you see into the water to watch where you're wading. They can help you spot fish too.

Gear for floating

Though parts of the Toccoa can be waded, many sections of the river are only fishable from some sort of watercraft. That may be because of water depth, distances involved, or river access or trespass concerns (or, in some cases, a combination of some or all of those factors).

Many Toccoa anglers like to float the river – so here's a brief look at some gear considerations if that describes you.

Float tubes: Float tubes can be useful on certain sections of the Toccoa. For instance, many find that the Delayed Harvest water offers good float tubing opportunities. Similarly, a tube can be used for *short* floats on the tailwater (for example, from the dam to Tammen Park or from Horseshoe Bend to Toccoa River Park). But note that float tubes are *not suitable* for longer floats on the tailwater. *Under no circumstances should you attempt one of the longer tailwater floats in a float tube.* Do *not* use float tubes for trips from Tammen Park to Curtis Switch or from Curtis Switch to Horseshoe Bend. Those extended floats are simply too long.

Similarly, note that the upper Toccoa is not float tube water either. Reasons include water depth, length of float, and (as we'll soon see) trespassing concerns.

On any river, use only a round, donut-shaped tube (never a U-shaped tube) – and when fishing from a float tube, *always wear your PFD.*

Personal pontoons: Some Toccoa anglers enjoy fishing the river from personal pontoons. Such watercraft have become increasingly popular in recent years, and a dedicated cadre of fly fishers likes to use them on the Toccoa tailwater...even for the longer floats. One reason for this popularity is that such craft have *oars*, and that allows you to row through slow stretcehes of river that might otherwise slow you down too much.

If you choose to use a personal pontoon, be sure that you fully understand how to use it on moving water and that you are able to handle any river hazards you may encounter while on the water. And (again) *always wear your PFD.*

Canoe, kayak, drift boat or raft: If you have a drift boat or raft with a rowing frame, and know how to safely manage it, you'll find that such a watercraft really opens up the Toccoa. Depending on water level, much of the Toccoa is suitable for fishing from a raft or drift boat. In fact, that's about the only way to fish much of the tailwater.

A word on "floating smart": It should go without saying, but don't attempt to float the tailwater in any sort of watercraft unless you understand all river use regulations, including those addressing wading and private property and trespass; unless you are completely familiar with possible hazards on the river; and unless you have the skills to undertake such a float. This book is *not* a boating guide in any sense and does not make any attempt to cover rivercraft, either generally or specifically as it applies to the Toccoa. You can find such information in a variety of paddling guides.

Be sure you fully understand what you're getting into if you plan a float on the Toccoa. You must always remember that you are completely responsible for your own safety and wellbeing (as well as for understanding and following all laws and regulations relating to river use, private property and trespass) when enjoying this or any other river.

Choosing the right flies

Some thoughts to help you select the best flies for your next Toccoa adventure.

Most of the anglers you see on the Toccoa tailwater will be fly fishers, and it's easy to understand why. This is a river with a *lot* of insect activity, and that's one thing that makes it a perfect place for fishing with a fly rod.

But exactly which flies should you use?

The answer to that seemingly simple question depends on a number of factors, including where and when you happen to be fishing. On this river, though, it often boils down to more or less matching the hatch.

The ability to match what's hatching can play a key role in your success on the Toccoa. These fish get to look at a lot of natural insects, and they can become selective at times. Thus, you've got to be equipped with the right flies to give them what they're looking for.

But how do you decide what the "right" flies are? I'm glad you asked!

The bug chart

There are many Toccoa hatch charts out there... and you'll find an even larger number of opinions (from some extremely knowledgeable anglers) on what flies will work best as well as on when and where you should use them.

Here, we'll try to combine and distill some of those diverse insights into what we'll call the "bug chart."

Our Toccoa bug chart (which you'll find on the next two pages) is a little different from some other hatch charts you may have seen. Instead of being keyed only to the *names* of bugs (for instance, "Green Drake"), it's tied to what you might actually *see* on the water (in that particular instance, a greenish mayfly).

Why this approach? Because even though you may not know you're

Common bugs on the Toccoa

On the Toccoa, knowing which bug you're seeing can help you pick the right imitation. Here's how to identify the insects you may see flying, with general suggestions on imitating adult and subsurface forms. For specific seasonal suggestions, see the bug chart on the next two pages.

Mayfly: The elegant little bug you see in magazines.
- Upswept wings
- Tapered abdomen
- Graceful tail

To imitate adult: Quill Gordon, Blue Winged Olive, Green Drake, Light Cahill
To imitate nymph: Pheasant Tail Nymph, Gold Ribbed Hare's Ear

Caddisfly: As plain as the mayfly is elegant.
- Swept-back wings held tent-like over abdomen

To imitate adult: Elk Hair Caddis, Stimulator
To imitate larva/pupa: Pheasant Tail Nymph, Sparkle Pupa

Stonefly: Resembles a caddisfly but holds wings flat.
- Some resemblance to the caddisfly but carries wings flat, not tentlike

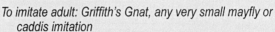

To imitate adult: Yellow Sally, Elk Hair Caddis
To imitate larva/pupa: Yellow or Black Stonefly Nymph, Pat's Rubber Legs

Midge: These are the tiny bugs!
- Very small
- Wings often flat

To imitate adult: Griffith's Gnat, any very small mayfly or caddis imitation
To imitate larva/pupa: Brassie, WD40, Zebra Midge, Midge Pupa

The Toccoa "bug chart"

If you see...	J	F	M	A	M	J	J	A	S	O	N	D
Midges	X									X	X	X
Black Caddis	X	X	X									
Black Stoneflies	X	X									X	X
Gray Caddis		X	X									
Grayish Mayflies *Quill Gordon*			X									
Olive Green Mayflies *Blue Winged Olive*			X	X						X	X	X
Brownish Green Mayflies *March Brown, Hendrickson*				X	X							
Gray/Brown Mayflies *Quill Gordon*				X	X							
Olive Caddis				X	X							
Yellowish Mayflies *Sulphurs*				X	X	X						
Small Yellow Stoneflies					X							
Greenish Mayflies *Green Drake*					X							
Ants					X	X	X	X	X			
Cream Mayflies *Light Cahill*						X	X	X	X			
Tan Caddis						X	X	X	X			
Yellow Mayflies *Yellow Drake*							X	X	X			
Hoppers and Beetles							X	X	X	X		
Brownish Orange Caddis *October Caddis*										X		

This chart indicates what you might see on the tailwater at various times of year and offers suggestions on patterns to might use to match the hatch.

Try these dries...	...or subsurface flies	Size
Parachute midge, Griffith's Gnat	Brassie, WD40, Midge Pupa	20-24
Black Elk Hair Caddis	Pheasant Tail Nymph	14-18
Dark Stonefly	Black Stonefly Nymph, Pat's Rubber Legs	16-18
Gray Elk Hair Caddis	Caddis Pupa, Pheasant Tail	14-18
Quill Gordon, Blue Dun	Pheasant Tail Nymph	14-16
Blue Winged Olive	Pheasant Tail Nymph	20-24
March Brown, Dark Hendrickson	Dark Hare's Ear, Pheasant Tail	14-16
Quill Gordon	Grayish Hare's Ear, Pheasant Tail	14-16
Olive Elk Hair Caddis	Olive Caddis Pupae, Olive Hare's Ear, Olive Pheasant Tail	16
Sulphur Comparadun	Sulphur Nymph, Pheasant Tail	16-18
Yellow Sally or Elk Hair Caddis	Yellow Stonefly Nymph	16
Green Drake	Green Drake Nymph, Pheasant Tail	10-12
Black Parachute Ant	Black Fur or Hardbodied Ant	14-18
Light Cahill	Light Cahill Nymph, Hare's Ear	14
Tan Elk Hair Caddis	Caddis Pupa, Tan Hare's Ear	14-18
Yellow Cahill, Tan Cahill	Yellow Drake Nymph, Hare's Ear	12-14
Stimulator, Dave's Hopper, Madame X, Beetle w/legs	Usually fished on surface	6-12
October Caddis	Caddis Pupa, Pheasant Tail Nymph	12-14

When matching the hatch:
Color, profile, or size?

You're fishing the tailwater and see a bug that you're able to identify as a tan-colored mayfly that's about a size 14. You've got several possible imitations in your fly box. One is the right color, one is the right profile, and one is the right size. Which should you choose?

Most agree that size is the most important consideration. A buggy-looking fly of the right size is often all it takes to fool a fish. Profile is usually ranked second, while color often ranks only a distant third.

On streams such as the Toccoa, where there may be relatively many hatches and where fish can become selective, there will be times when you must consider all three qualities to come up with the right fly for that particular day.

The bottom line: Go prepared with a well-stocked fly box, using the hatch chart as well as up-to-the-minute info from local fly shops or other anglers to help you refine your selection.

seeing a "Green Drake," you *will* know you're seeing a greenish mayfly and can then choose your fly accordingly.

The chart can be used as a starting point no matter where on the Toccoa you're fishing. It also shows times of year when various bugs are likely to be seen and further notes specific flies that you can use to imitate those insects. Suggestions for specific topwater (dry) as well as subsurface (nymph/larva/emerger) flies are also provided. But note that there are *many* different flies which can be used to imitate most of the insects that you see. If you don't have the specified fly in your box, don't despair. Instead, just go with some other pattern of similar size and profile. Often that will work out just fine.

Putting the bug chart to work

To see how you might use the bug chart, let's look at an example. Assume that you're fishing during May and see bugs of some sort flying above the water. After catching one and taking a close look, you decide it's an greenish looking caddisfly. From the chart, you decide to imitate it with an olive Elk Hair Caddis. Further, you learn that you can imitate its subsurface form with an olive Hare's Ear Nymph, an olive Pheasant Tail Nymph, or even an olive Caddis Pupae of some sort.

But what if you don't see bug activity? Don't worry. Even though you may not see flying adults, there's still subsurface activity going on. Immature insects (nymphs, larvae and so on) are almost always active, and the bug chart will help you make an informed guess as what patterns to start with at various times. You can even look under rocks to see what's moving and then match its general form and size.

But remember that hatch charts are not carved in stone. Bugs may appear earlier or later than shown. On that May day in question, for instance, you might do well with Yellow Sallies (to imitate small yellow stoneflies), with yellowish Comparaduns (to imitate yellowish mayflies), with Green Drakes (to imitate greenish mayflies) or if its already warming up perhaps even with Fur Ants.

The moral? Carry a good selection of flies when fishing the Toccoa. Be prepared for a variety of fly-selection challenges, and you'll be well on your way to catching more Toccoa trout.

Some Toccoa strategies

The foregoing will help you figure out what fly to start with. But on the Toccoa it can sometimes get a little more complicated. Here's a look at how to handle some of the situations you might encounter.

Use multiple flies to increase your odds of success

On the Toccoa, there are often several different types of insects active

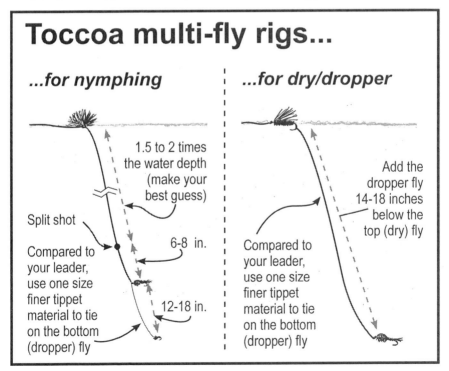

at any given time. The fish are seeing a diverse buffet of sizes, shapes and forms of bugs and can easily become selective. When that happens, you can increase your odds of success by offering them several different options to choose from.

The way to do this is with a multi-fly or "dropper" rig that lets you offer multiple flies at the same time. By mixing and matching, you can simultaneously present imitations that mimic more than one type of insect or more than one insect form (for example, an adult or an emerger). Hopefully, one of them will do the job.

One popular multi-fly set-up for the Toccoa is a two-nymph rig consisting of a size 14 Pheasant Tail Nymph paired with a small midge (perhaps a Brassie, Zebra Midge or WD-40) in size 18 to 22. Though the fish undoubtedly notice both flies, they may focus on and take only one.

Another possibility is a dry/dropper combo that combines a surface (floating) fly with a sinking (subsurface) fly. On the Toccoa, try pairing a size 14 tan Elk Hair Caddis dry with a size 16 Pheasant Tail Nymph. This can be a great combination in riffle water, and fish may hit either fly. It's effective in other types of water too.

Lots of bugs...active fish...but you can't get a strike!

Here's a challenge that's frequently encountered on the Toccoa during caddisfly season in the spring. You'll see clouds of caddis on the river, and there may be lots of splashing on the water. Given all of that excitement, you might figure that all you have to do to catch fish is to use a dry such as an Elk Hair Caddis. So you try it – but you get nothing. In fact, you can't get a strike "for love nor money," as my granddad used to say... even though all around you the trout are feeding on *something!*

What may be happening is that the fish are ignoring the winged adults (and thus your high-floating Elk Hair Caddis dry) but are chowing down on near-surface but still subsurface forms (that is, on emergers) instead.

If this happens to you, clip off the dry fly and switch to something that imitates a *subsurface* version of whatever bugs you see flying. In this case, try a soft-hackled emerger or a Pheasant Tail Nymph. You can fish it deep (like a nymph) or shallow (like an emerger). Often that simple change is all it takes to turn your luck around.

Drag-free...or not

On a recent Toccoa trip, a friend and I were fishing the tailwater several miles below Blue Ridge Dam. We were wading and having a good day fishing nymphs. However, we were using those nymphs in an

Streamers: The year-round flies

There are some *large* fish in the Toccoa. Yes, they will sometimes eat tiny bugs. But while big fish like a light snack now and then, what really gets 'em going is a *big* meal like a nice, fat minnow – and the way to imitate minnows is with streamers.

Toccoa River guide Jake Darling, of Unicoi Outfitters in nearby Helen, Ga., is enthusiastic about the possibilities of streamer fishing on the Toccoa.

"These trout like to chase things down," he says, adding that streamers such as the Sparkle Minnow (in tan and olive with flash) or the Sculpzilla (in white or in tan/orange) make great targets.

"But I don't know that it's pattern as much as it's color," Jake says. His favorite color for the Toccoa is generally some shade of tan, perhaps because that makes for an effective sculpin imitation. If conditions are bright he favors tan or yellow, but if it's a dull day he often goes with darker shades or even black.

How about the weight of his streamers? "I prefer a lightweight streamer to get the most lifelike motion in the water," he says. Relatively lightweight flies tend to move horizontally instead of up and down, he notes, just as a natural minnow tends to move.

Jake prefers a sink-tip line when fishing streamers. Leader-wise, he goes with a short 4- to 5-foot leader to help him stay in touch with the fly.

How to fish streamers on the Toccoa: After making your cast (typically toward some sort of cover where large fish may be holding), position your rod low so it's pointing down your line towards the fly...and then strip the streamer back to you, varying the speed and length of the strips to find out what's working. Strikes are often hard and unmistakable.

"There's nothing like it," Jake adds. "On the Toccoa, streamer fishing can provide the best bite in the game."

Jake Darling with a nice Toccoa trout.

Photo courtesy Unicoi Outfitters

unusual way – starting with a drag-free drift but ending by letting the nymphs hang in the current for a moment before actively stripping them upstream using short, fast tugs.

It was the opposite of a drag-free drift, but it was working!

Here's how to try this technique yourself. During the main part of your drift, go for as much of a drag-free presentation as possible. But then change things up at the *end* of the drift by allowing the fly to hang in the current for a few moments. Just let it sit there. As you do, the fly will tend to ride upwards as it planes toward the surface.

And then add icing to the cake by stripping the nymph toward you.

Why does this work? To the fish, it apparently appears that your fly is a nymph or an emerger that's dashing for the surface. The fish can't stand to let it get away and so nails it with what's often a very hard strike. It can be a very effective technique.

You're getting refusals...

When the Toccoa fish are active on the surface, it's not unusual find that fish are coming up to look at your fly but then turning away at the last minute. What's going on, and how do you fix it?

Assuming that you've got a good drag-free drift, and also assuming that you're not spooking the fish with sudden movement or some other alarming behavior, refusals of that sort often mean that you've got the right pattern but the wrong size.

Try downsizing one or two sizes to see if that makes a difference.

Try terrestrials during summer and fall

As spring gives way to summer, the buggy mix on the Toccoa becomes even more diverse as "terrestrials" enter the picture. These include beetles, grasshoppers, crickets and the like – bugs that live on land but that occasionally find themselves in the water.

Terrestrial appearances are not subject to the whim of hatch schedules. Instead, they're available pretty much all summer long. That means they can work even when the traditional bugs aren't hatching.

Though trout seem surprisingly fond of terrestrials, relatively few anglers use terrestrial imitations on trout streams. But they should! During the heat of summer, try big, juicy looking flies such as Turk's Tarantula as well as smaller offerings like size 14 deer hair beetles or size 18 ants. Put these flies close to cover (that is, close to places where a real bug might lose its footing and fall in). The result may be a big strike as a trout appears from nowhere and hammers your fly.

While we're talking about fishing the Toccoa with terrestrials, there's one other secret class of flies that really should be mentioned – and that's the foam spider.

What? Foam spiders for trout? Yes indeed – and perhaps even popping bugs too! Remember that the trout see a spider or a popper just as a bream sees it – as a chunky-looking something that's probably good to eat. The trout doesn't know (and apparently doesn't care) that the popper was tied for bream and so nails it with wild abandon.

Try one of these out-of-the-ordinary offerings sometime during the summer. The true purist may look at you a little strangely, but that look just might change if a big trout makes the water blow up as it blasts the fly.

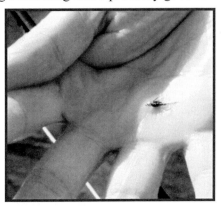

Small nymphs like this little Pheasant Tail often mean big fish on the Toccoa. Just be sure that you're fishing them deep.

Fine-tuning for wintertime

The Toccoa is open for fishing all year long, and during the cold months you'll want to make some adjustments in your fly selection.

During winter on the Toccoa, as on many streams, there'll be times when you need to go with midges – the flies that anglers love to hate. Yes, they're small...size 24 or 26 or possibly smaller. They're hard to tie to tippet (especially when it's cold), and it's hard to believe that any fly as diminutive as that could ever hook and hold a fish. But they do, and you'll want to add them to your wintertime fly box for sure.

But don't overlook the possibilities offered by more familiar flies during winter. Try what guide David Hulsey calls "the holy trifecta" of wintertime tailwater flies: the Pheasant Tail, Gold Ribbed Hare's Ear, and Prince Nymph. Try small versions in sizes 16 or 18.

The junk food gambit

Finally, if you find yourself fishing over recently stocked fish, you may encounter one of those situations where the fish simply turn up their collective noses at your carefully tied classic trout flies.

Why? Possibly because they want "junk food" instead!

So-called "junk food" flies include egg imitations (like Y2Ks and

Sucker Spawn) plus San Juan Worms and other worm imitations. These flies appeal strongly to a trout's built-in willingness to eat eggy- or wormy-looking things, so they can be effective on newly stocked fish who haven't yet learned about all of those other tasty things in the river.

The term "junk fly" is an unfortunate one, for the eggs or aquatic worms which these flies imitate are natural parts of the diet of any trout. Thus, you can fish with such flies while comfortable in the knowledge that you really are presenting imitations of natural foods.

Junk flies can be very important on the Delayed Harvest section of the Toccoa, especially when fishing over newly-stocked fish. Fresh stockers may still be learning about hatches, but they'll often go for an egg or worm in a heartbeat. We'll talk more about this in the section on Delayed Harvest.

A tailwater fly selection challenge

Picking flies for turnover

Sometime in October, as Blue Ridge Lake's surface water cools, the lake will experience "turnover." That happens when surface water becomes cooler than the deeper water and thus sinks.

Turnover produces several weeks of cloudy water in the tailwater below the dam. This sudden cloudiness definitely impacts fishing; in fact, following turnover, the action will slow for three or four weeks until the water clears.

But you can still catch fish.

One tactic for turnover is to switch to very high-visibility flies. This is a good time to consider relatively garish patterns such as a hot pink San Juan Worm, a Y2K, or a peach or pink Egg or Sucker Spawn fly. Such flies are simply easier for fish to see in murky water. Fish 'em deep with plenty of weight just as you would fish a nymph.

Keep at it till you figure it out!

Regardless of the time of year, and despite even the most sophisticated of hatch charts, one thing you'll quickly learn about Toccoa hatches is that it's not always easy to figure them out.

For example: One day you may have a banner day with an Elk Hair Caddis and a Soft-Hackle Caddis Emerger as a dropper. But the next day you won't get a second look even though you're using the exact same flies that worked so well just 24 hours earlier.

It can get a little maddening at times, but sometimes that's just part of the fun of fishing the Toccoa!

Part 2: Upper Toccoa

Deep Hole to Sandy Bottom

- Finding and accessing the upper Toccoa
- "Can I fish here?"
- How maps can help you figure out upper Toccoa fishability
- Choosing the right flies for the upper Toccoa
- Upper Toccoa techniques

Upper Toccoa River

From Deep Hole to Sandy Bottom, there's 13.8 miles of water, a bunch of private land, and a set of access and river use rules that can make you crazy. But if you can find the right places...

From a fishing point of view, the Toccoa can be divided into three sections: the upper Toccoa (Deep Hole to Sandy Bottom), the middle "Delayed Harvest" portion (Sandy Bottom down to near Shallowford Bridge); and the tailwater (Blue Ridge Dam to the town of McCaysville).

Let's look first at the upper Toccoa, beginning at the U.S. Forest Service's Deep Hole Recreation Area (off GA 60 and FS-293) and going downriver to the Sandy Bottom canoe takeout on Old Dial Road. There's also about 10 miles of headwaters above that section, but private land makes that upper-upper water all but inaccessible.

The stretch from Deep Hole to Sandy Bottom has been designated as the Toccoa River Canoe Trail, the only such canoe trail in the Chattahoochee-Oconee National Forest. It includes 13.8 miles of river, mostly Class I or II water but occasionally rougher. It's a very scenic waterway, well suited for a float in a canoe, kayak or raft or shallow-draft drift boat.

Since this isn't a canoeing guide, we won't go into the upper Toccoa canoeing experience (but check The Georgia Canoeing Association website at www.gapaddle.com). Instead, we'll talk about fishing...and on the upper Toccoa, that means we're going to be talking about access.

"Can I fish here?" Maybe...but maybe not...

You might reasonably think that since the upper Toccoa is a designated canoe trail, fishing along it would be a straightforward affair.

The author with a nice upper Toccoa rainbow. This one went for a streamer fished through the top of a deep run.

But in reality it gets very complicated. Why? Because this section of the river flows through a patchwork of some public and a lot of private land. Since the land is a mix of public and private, special considerations dictate how recreational users, including fishermen, can use the river. Those special considerations *must* be kept in mind.

Here's the word from the U.S. Forest Service website as of late 2014:

> **Those persons floating the Toccoa River are allowed passage through private lands along the river. However, according to state law, fishing, camping and entering onto private land is illegal without landowner permission, <u>as is fishing from the river in a boat, tube, or any other floating device where both sides of the river are privately owned</u> [emphasis added].**

Land ownership is taken seriously in this neck of the woods, and it's best to err on the side of caution. If you're not sure about the status of a particular section of river, don't wade or fish it.

To summarize the fishing situation on the upper Toccoa:

- If both sides of river are National Forest, you can wade and fish.
- If both sides of river are private land, you *cannot* wade (that is, you can't touch the bottom) and you *cannot* fish at all.

Things become even more complicated where one side of the river is National Forest but the other is privately owned. In those areas, Georgia law generally says that the landowner owns the stream bottom out to the centerline of the flow, unless the deed specifically states otherwise.

More info can be found at the U.S. Forest Service website:

http://www.fs.usda.gov/recarea/conf/recreation/hiking/recarea/?recid=10536&actid=79

Deciding what's what and where's where on the upper Toccoa

As you might guess, questions of what you can and cannot do (and where you can and cannot do it) are enough to discourage many anglers from fishing the upper Toccoa. However, there is some National Forest along this stretch of river. Thus, the potential for fishing remains – if you're willing to take time to figure out what's what and where's where.

Fortunately, as Toccoa River guide Jake Darling notes, it's sometimes easy to pick out much of the non-National-Forest land

"It's often pretty easy to tell what is and is not National Forest," Jake says. "If you see pastures, vacation homes, or lawns, you'll know you're looking at private land. It's not hard to identify."

Another thing that can be helpful is the presence of signs marking of National Forest boundaries (and, in some cases, signs identifying private property). Signage is clear in some areas. But whether or not any particular boundary is marked, the responsibility to know where you are (and to know the status of land around you) is still yours.

Getting help from maps

If you want to fish this upper stretch, a good starting point will be a good map of the Chattahoochee-Oconee National Forest. Such a map will help you identify National Forest boundaries in order to pinpoint areas of the river that you can fish under the current guidelines.

Such maps are available from a number of different sources, including the U.S. Forest Service's webstore. Here's that store's web address:

www.fs.fed.us/recreation/nationalforeststore/

The map on pages 36-37, based on Forest Service maps, shows the upper Toccoa from Deep Hole to Sandy Bottom and shows approximate National Forest boundaries. Areas designated as National Forest are shown in gray; white areas indicate private land. Just remember to take no chances with private land. If in doubt, don't trespass.

For even more detail, you might want to check out the on-line map that's available from the U.S. Forest Service. Here's where to find it:

www.fs.usda.gov/Internet/FSE_DOCUMENTS/fsm9_028893.pdf

As you explore this map, note that the white areas are private land, while green areas are National Forest. Also note the "zoom" feature which helps you locate roads, trails, gates and other features that may figure into your planning. However, not all Forest Service roads are open to vehicles all of the time. Some roads are gated and may be closed to vehicles, though you can still use them as hiking routes for foot access.

If you do decide to explore and fish the upper Toccoa on your own, it's a good idea to print a copy of any relevant maps to take with you. You might even be able to access suitable maps on your GPS.

Floating the upper Toccoa

As you have no doubt realized, floating the Upper Toccoa (that is, floating the Toccoa River Canoe Trail) does not open up nearly as much water to fishing as you might expect it to. Nonetheless, some fly fishers enjoy floating this stretch and simply limit their fishing to the areas where fishing is not in conflict with river use regulations.

Those who float the upper Toccoa can access the river at two official Forest Service access points – the Deep Hole Recreation Area and the Sandy Bottoms Recreation area.

The Deep Hole Recreation Area provides access on the upstream end. Located just a short distance off GA 60 via FS-293, this area features a limited number of campsites available on a first-come, first-served basis (no reservations) for a small per-night fee. There are no electric hookups and no water (and no dump station). But there is a restroom, plus picnic tables and a fishing platform. A small day-use parking fee is charged.

On-line Forest Service maps can help you figure out access routes and also help you determine whether various sections of the upper Toccoa are open to fishing.

By the way, there really is a "deep hole" at Deep Hole. It's located right in front of the canoe launch (and just downstream from a fish stocking station).

To reach Deep Hole from Blue Ridge, Ga., take US 515 north for 4 miles to GA 60 and turn right. Follow GA 60 through Morganton (for about 2 miles) and then turn right to stay on GA 60. Continue another 14.8 miles to the Deep Hole area, which will be on your right. It's clearly marked by a prominent sign.

On the downstream end, the canoe trail ends at the Sandy Bottom Recreation Area. It offers facilities similar to those at Deep Hole, including limited first-come, first-serve camping and day use parking.

To reach Sandy Bottom from Blue Ridge, Ga., go south on Aska Road for 8.5 miles to Shallowford Bridge. Turn left and go across Shallowford Bridge, then make a right turn onto Shallowford Bridge Road. Continue for 1.3 miles to Old Dial Road. Turn right on Old Dial Road and go another 0.6 miles to recreation area, which will be on your right.

On the upper Toccoa, as on other rivers, access is only part of the equation. Another part is water level. You'll want to be sure there's enough water so you're not dragging over every shallow spot you see. Check the gauge at Dial (it's downriver of the Sandy Bottom put-in) by going to **www.tva.com/lakes/streams.htm** and scrolling down to "Toccoa near Dial." Look at the second parameter, "flow," which tells you how much water is flowing in the river. Most river users feel that you need at least 350 cfs on the Dial gauge for a good float. Interestingly, as we'll see, that same figure (350 cfs) is usually considered the upper limit for safe wading below Sandy Bottom.

If you're making a float trip on this section of the Toccoa, the biggest problem (aside from those complicated access issues already noted) may well be the matter of pacing yourself so that you reach your takeout point. It's a *long* float from one end of the canoe trail to the other, and if you take too much time fishing or sightseeing along the way it's easy to run out of time and daylight before you run out of river.

For that reason, many upper Toccoa float enthusiasts will break up the run and float only part of it at a time...or find an intermediate put-in or take out to make a shorter run possible. Some private access points may be available at times and for a fee; check with area fly shops or canoe outfitters to see if there's such an alternate access might be available to allow you to plan a shorter trip.

What about tubing the upper Toccoa?

Can you float the upper Toccoa in a float tube? Generally speaking, no. This float is simply too long. Besides, you'd have to walk your tube through a lot of shallow areas...and that would not only slow you even more but would inevitably mean walking (trespassing) on private land (since you'd be walking on, and not floating over, the bottom).

So scratch the idea of doing the upper Toccoa in a float tube. If you want to float this section, use a canoe, a kayak, or some other suitable boat instead.

Boaters will find two public access points to the Toccoa River Canoe Trail. There's access at the upstream end at Deep Hole (above) and downstream at Sandy Bottom (right).

The upper Toccoa without a boat

What if you don't have a boat? Is there foot-accessible public fishing on the upper Toccoa?

Yes, there is. Though much of the land along the upper Toccoa is private, it's possible in some places to approach this water on foot by hiking across public land. This offers the possibility of river access to footbound anglers who are willing to figure out where the public land is...especially if said anglers are willing to do some walking.

There's foot access at the Deep Hole canoe launch, where you'll find some nice wadable water. Expect to find fish there, too – there's even a fish stocking station just upstream of the canoe launch!

Similarly, there's wadable water at Sandy Bottom. In fact, the Delayed Harvest section of the Toccoa extends for 450 feet upstream from the Sandy Bottom take-out, and you'll find good wading there.

If you don't mind some hiking, there's another intriguing wading possibility where the Benton Mackaye Trail crosses the river (on a swinging bridge, no less). To reach the bridge, follow GA 60 to FS-816, a gravel road. Follow FS-816 for 3.1 miles to its end. There, a short connector trail continues beyond the road and almost immediately intersects the Benton Mackaye Trail (diamond blazes) which you'll follow for about a quarter mile to the river. There's some wading near the bridge crossing. But even if you don't fish, just experiencing the bridge is worth the hike.

In foot-accessible areas like these, always remember the unwritten but oh-so-true motto of exploration-minded anglers everywhere: The more you're willing to walk, the better the fishing is likely to be.

If you are conscientious in your planning, it's definitely possible to fish the upper Toccoa on foot. But you have to do your homework before

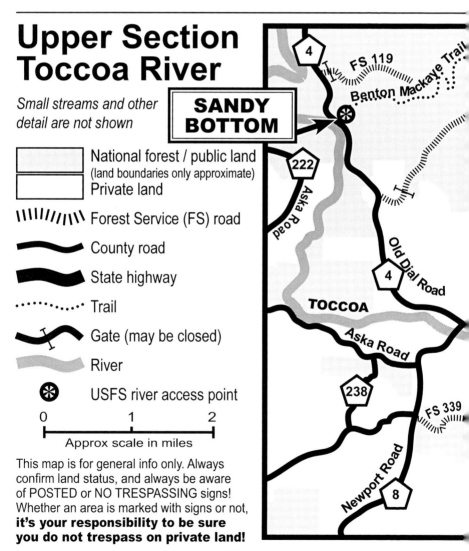

you go...and you must be *sure* you know where the property boundaries are. If you don't feel up to that challenge, then you're probably better off fishing a different part of the river.

Upper Toccoa fly fishing strategies

What can you expect fishing-wise from this portion of the river? You'll find that the fishing here can be enjoyable for several reasons. For one, it's surprisingly big water with ample room for casting. For another, it usually holds fish.

Though a limited amount of natural reproduction takes place on this stretch,

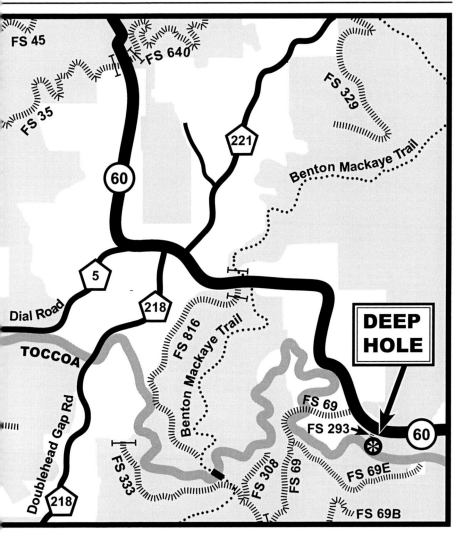

this fishery relies to a large extent on stocking. It also benefits from stockings in some of its major tributaries (specifically, Rock Creek and Coopers Creek), two of the most heavily stocked streams in the state. Stocked fish wandering downstream in those tributaries may end up in the upper Toccoa.

Additionally, wild fish from other tributaries may also make their way into the Toccoa – and some trout hold over from year to year too. Those holdovers, who handle summer heat by taking refuge in deep, cool holes, can reach surprising sizes.

You'll find that the upper Toccoa fishes best from late fall through early summer – when the water is cool, in other words, and when it's not too low.

There's wadable water near the swinging bridge which carries the Benton Mackaye Trail over the river.

Later, during the summer, water levels will usually drop and water temperatures will rise. That adversely impacts the trout prospects during warmer parts of the year, though warmer-water species love it.

A favorite time is spring, for spring brings abundant bug life to the upper Toccoa. Springtime hatches can be good ones. Make an effort to match the hatch for best results, though along this section you'll often do just fine with general purpose attractors such as the Royal Wulff or the Stimulator.

Particularly in the lower portion toward Sandy Bottom, you might even try targeting smallmouth bass. Use brown or black woolly buggers, crawfish imitations, popping bugs, or streamers – including the venerable Clouser Minnow. The Clouser, you'll recall, was originally developed as a smallmouth bass fly for use in Pennsylvania. It works on Georgia smallmouth too.

Since the upper Toccoa is not a tailwater but is instead a freeflowing stream, its level is determined by precipitation and runoff within the watershed. That means that you don't have to worry about sudden rises in the river's level like you do on the tailwater portion of the Toccoa below Blue Ridge Dam.

Part 3: Delayed Harvest Water

Sandy Bottom to end of Delayed Harvest section

- Delayed Harvest overview
- Finding and accessing the DH section
- "Is it wadable today?"
- Should you wade or float?
- Choosing the right flies for the Toccoa DH
- Cold-weather techniques

Toccoa River delayed harvest

Here's how to enjoy the special-regs "Delayed Harvest" section of the Toccoa River

The Toccoa River Canoe Trail ends at the Sandy Bottom take-out off Old Dial Road. But for many Toccoa fly fishing enthusiasts, that's where fun *begins* – because Sandy Bottom marks the jumping-in point for the Toccoa's exciting Delayed Harvest section.

What is Delayed Harvest? In Georgia, as elsewhere, there are a number of creeks and rivers that teeter on the edge when comes to being cold enough for trout. During summer and early fall, when the weather is hot, those streams are too warm for trout. However, once cooler weather arrives and water temperatures start to fall, it isn't long until those same streams reach temperatures that are much more to the trout's liking.

To take advantage of that shift in water temperatures, Georgia has established a Delayed Harvest season for certain waters in the state. There are currently five designated delayed harvest

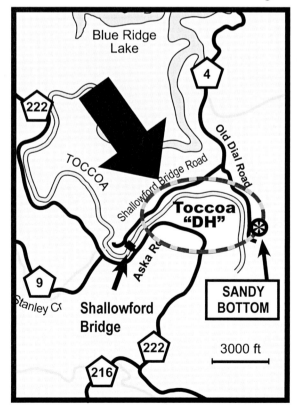

Guide David Hulsey of Southern Highroads Outfitters with a nice Toccoa River Delayed Harvest rainbow.

waters in the state, and one of them is the DH section of the Toccoa.

This special season runs from Nov. 1 through May 14. During that "DH season," as it's called, special regulations apply:
- 100% catch-and-release
- Artificials only
- Single-hook lures only (but droppers are okay)

While spin fishing is allowed on DH waters (as long as the single-hook, artificials-only, and catch-and-release rules are followed), most of the anglers that you encounter during the DH season will be fly fishers.

An overview of the Toccoa Delayed Harvest section

The Toccoa DH is the most recent of Georgia's five DH fisheries. The idea for adding it was suggested by the Blue Ridge Chapter of Trout Unlimited. With good water quality and lots of trout-friendly habitat, it looked like an ideal candidate for inclusion in the DH program. And because the entire stretch flows through public land, it also came without the access challenges that have been an issue on other sections of the Toccoa.

It all came together in November of 2006 when this section of the Toccoa became Georgia's fifth Delayed Harvest stream. All in all, it's what one angler recently called "a totally satisfying bit of water."

The Toccoa DH begins just above Sandy Bottom and continues for about 1.3 miles downstream. Here's the description of the boundaries of this section straight from the Georgia Department of Natural Resources:

> ...from 0.4 miles above Shallowford Bridge upstream to a point 450 feet upstream of the Sandy Bottom Canoe Access.

Accessing the DH water

River access is easy on the Toccoa DH because of its close proximity to two well-maintained gravel roads –Shallowford Bridge Road and Old

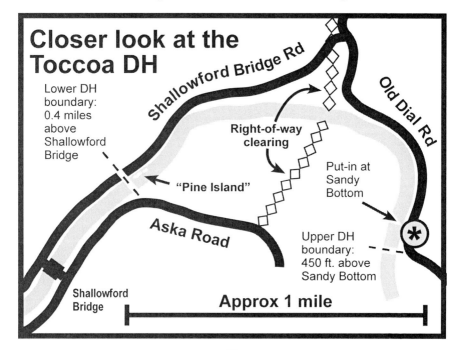

Dial Road. At either end of the DH stretch the river runs near the road; in the middle section, it swings away from the road a bit and some walking will be required to reach the water.

A primary access point is the Sandy Bottom recreation area and canoe access near the upriver end of the Toccoa DH. Sandy Bottom features a parking area with room for a number of cars; a small parking fee is charged. There are also a number of campsites which are available on a first-come, first-served basis (also for a per-night fee).

You'll also find plenty of access downriver from Sandy Bottom. Below the canoe launch area, parking will be limited to wide spots on the shoulder of the road. There are a number of obvious parking spots along the two roads, but they're invariably small. Most have room for only a couple of vehicles at most.

Because of the limited parking, it's a courtesy to your fellow anglers to pull well off the road when parking. Pull forward, too, so as to leave room for someone else. In other words, don't park in the middle of a two-car-sized area, since that could make it impossible for another fly fisher to park there too.

Remember that parking pullouts usually signal river access. Some pullouts are only a few steps from the water, while others position you to follow paths or trails.

One other river access possibility – a trail which follows a power line right-of-way – is worth mentioning. This trail begins where Shallowford

Finding the Toccoa DH

Here's how to get to the lower end of the Toccoa Delayed Harvest section.

- From Blue Ridge, follow Aska Road for about 8.4 miles to Shallowford Bridge Road, which will be on your left.
- Turn left to cross Shallowford Bridge (a one-lane bridge) over the Toccoa.
- At the end of the bridge, go right and follow the river upstream. The downstream end of the Toccoa Delayed Harvest water is 0.4 miles from the end of Shallowford Bridge.

From that point, here's how to reach the uppermost DH access at the Sandy Bottom Canoe Launch area:

- After crossing the river as described above, continue to follow Shallowford Bridge Road beyond the end of Shallowford Bridge to Old Dial Road.
- Turn right and follow Old Dial Road for 0.7 miles to the Sandy Bottom Recreation Area.

The Delayed Harvest section begins 450 feet upstream from the Sandy Bottom canoe access.

Photo courtesy James Bradley

Fishing the upper end of the Toccoa DH just downriver from the Sandy Bottom access point (visible in the background). At Sandy Bottom, a ramp on river right provides easy access from the parking area to the river.

Bridge Road intersects a power line right-of-way very close to Old Dial Road. The trail follows the right-of-way clearing downhill for several hundred yards to the river. Yes, some hiking will be required – but that may be a small price to pay for access to water that receives less pressure than do the more accessible stretches located closer to the road.

Wade or float?

Now that you know how to find the water, how will you fish it?

Most anglers you see on this section will be wading. Though some areas are definitely too deep for wading, many other stretches are shallow enough that wading is straightforward and sometimes even easy.

But wading is not the only way to fish this water. As long as the river level is suitable, the Toccoa DH is good water to fish from a raft, pontoon or float tube. But float only if you are certain you can do so safely – and when floating, always remember to wear your PFD.

It's possible to float the entire Toccoa DH, about 1.4 miles of water.

On the downstream end, the Toccoa Delayed Harvest water ends 0.4 miles above Shallowford Bridge, a single-lane bridge (shown at right) which carries Shallowford Bridge Road over the river.

That's not terribly long as floats go. A straight-through float goes quickly. However, stopping to fish will slow you down and make the trip last longer – particularly if you move around as you fish in order to explore the water thoroughly. Thus, you may want to allow as much as 3 to 4 hours (or more) to float and fish the entire stretch.

One excellent alternative to floating the whole thing is to float only the upper part of the DH section. "Upper," in this case, is arbitrarily defined as the section between Sandy Bottom (on the upstream end) and the power line right-of-way clearing on the lower end. When you reach the right-of-way clearing, exit river right. Then shoulder your float tube and hike up the hill back to the

> ### "Is it wadable today?"
>
> The Toccoa DH isn't impacted by releases from any dam. However, its level fluctuates with precipitation in the watershed. Sometimes it's wadable and sometimes it's not.
>
> To get an idea of whether the Toccoa DH is wadable, check the following TVA site:
>
> **www.tva.com/lakes/streams.htm**
>
> Then scroll down to "Toccoa near Dial" to see what the river is doing. The second parameter you'll see, "flow," tells you how much water is flowing in the river.
>
> The DH should only be waded at levels of 300 cfs or lower. If the flow is higher than that, wading becomes increasingly challenging. A few daring souls will wade certain areas up to about 350 cfs, but not me. I limit my wading to times when it's flowing at less than 300 cfs and suggest that you do the same. It's more fun that way...and a whole lot safer.

A solitary wading angler drifts a nymph through a promising run near the Sandy Bottom canoe access point. Similar runs are found throughout the Delayed Harvest section.

intersection of Shallowford Bridge and Old Dial Roads. From there, turn right and follow Old Dial Road back to Sandy Bottom. You may be able to do this several times in a day, exploring different runs and pools each time you make the float.

For a longer adventure, it's also possible to float the entire Delayed Harvest stretch. In that case, you'll start at Sandy Bottom and take out near the bottom end of the DH water. Of course, you could also start at the power line clearing and float only the lower portion.

A drift boat trip on the Toccoa DH can be an adventure you'll never forget. Here, guide David Hulsey positions an angler on a section of promising Delayed Harvest water.

In either of those cases, your float will end in the vicinity of what's been called the "Rock Garden" – a stretch of water that becomes increasingly rocky as you move downstream. Just above the Rock Garden is an extended area of deep water. Your cue that it's time to start thinking about exiting the river is a large, narrow, flat rock sticking up at an angle in the middle of the river. That rock is just about impossible to miss, and it's clearly visible from Shallowford Bridge Road too...making it easy to scout this section from the road before you make the float.

Once you spot the angled rock, start looking for two very small islands located near the river's right bank and begin to work your way to the right. The downstream island, often called Pine Island, is easily identified by a large pine tree which angles from the island out over the river.

You'll want to exit on the right side of the river somewhere above the first island since the water below that point becomes significantly rougher as it flows and drops through an area of rocky shoals. Some-

Float tubes are practical for use on the Toccoa DH and provide access to water that might be difficult to fish otherwise.

times the fishing can be good among those rocks, which do offer a lot of cover and holding water. However, maneuvering among them can be tricky depending on water level.

Beyond the islands and the Rock Garden you'll see houses built along the river and what is clearly private property. If you're floating, be sure that you exit the river while you can still do so on public land.

Finally, here's some float-related advice worth emphasizing: Be sure that you can recognize the takeout from the water and that you know how to get to it...and be sure that you have a plan for getting back to your vehicle once you're out of the river.

For those who want to neither wade nor float but prefer to fish from the bank, an informal network of trails provides dry-land anglers with access to much of the Delayed Harvest shoreline. Most shore fishing will be done by folks using casting gear, since bank-bound anglers will find

Put your flies where the fish are
Go deep for winter trout

Toccoa guide Jeff Turner, of Blue Ridge Fly Fishing, emphasizes the importance of make sure that you're fishing deep enough during the colder months on the Toccoa DH.

"You almost always have to fish way deeper than you think you do," Jeff says.

Jeff notes that many Toccoa DH fly fishers, especially those new to this river, think that they are getting their flies down deep where the fish are, while in reality the flies are actually drifting relatively high in the water column. Anglers tend to add weight based on the depth of the water they're fishing, but on the Toccoa the water is often so clear that you really don't appreciate just how deep a pool or run might be.

"There's deep water everywhere on the Toccoa," Jeff says, "and especially in the winter during most of the DH, that's where the fish are."

"There are a lot of fish in the Toccoa DH," he adds. "During the colder months, if you are not catching fish, then the odds are that you are not fishing deep enough."

casting room in short supply in most areas.

Choosing flies for DH

Now you're ready to put together a fly box for your Toccoa DH trip. You'd think it would be simple to choose flies for a bunch of stocked fish...but it can be more complicated than you think!

Here's why. Since Georgia's DH streams receive several stockings through the course

Photo courtesy Jeff Turner

A nice trout landed by Jeff Turner, who underscores the importance of using enough weight to get your subsurface flies such as nymphs down deep where the fish are.

of a typical DH season, there's a chance that at any given time you'll be fishing to two different kinds of fish: (1) "newbie" fish that have only recently been stocked and (2) "veteran" fish that have been in the river for a while.

The "newbie" fish, fresh from the hatchery, may still be driven primarily by their genetically programmed tendency to eat things that are (for example) eggy-looking or buggy-looking or that try to get away. When targeting such fish, you'll often do well using Y2K or Sucker Spawn egg imitations, buggy nymphs, or flashy, fast-moving streamers.

On the other hand, "veteran" fish from earlier stockings have had time to learn about all the other culinary opportunities that are found in the river. Yes, they'll still grab egg imitations and will usually pounce on streamers. But they have also discovered that their new home is loaded with lots of other good things to eat. Thus, they'll respond more like "wild" fish and may even become selective.

To catch such fish, you've got to give 'em what they want by matching the hatch, and (as we have seen) the Toccoa is a stream with a diverse buffet of bugs from which the fish can choose. Thus, the smart DH angler carries a well-stocked fly box to cover as many bases as possible.

The bug chart on pages 20-21 will give you an idea of the kinds of insects you might encounter at various times of year and will help you select appropriate imitations. But remember to carry tried-and-true stocked-trout standards such as egg and worm patterns too...and always be sure that you include some streamers!

Toccoa DH strategies

Interesting water is not hard to find on the Toccoa DH. You'll encounter runs, riffles, rapids, ledges, submerged boulders, brush-lined banks, deep holes and more – and any may hold fish.

The first water that many anglers see here is the great-looking run which flows directly in front of the Sandy Bottom canoe launch. Since this is a major access point, that particular run gets a good bit of pressure. But it often holds fish – and since there are lots more like it on this stretch, it serves as a good intro to a type of water that's common on the Toccoa DH.

Sometimes, in fact, you'll find areas that include many runs. Fishing such areas can be intimidating until you get the hang of them, but it's actually fairly straightforward. Just approach each run as if it was a small creek. Nymphs (or egg or worm imitations) can be very productive in such places, and streamers worked across or along edges can draw hard strikes as well. Also try a dry or a dry/dropper combo, floating it along the seams between the faster shoal water and the slower runs. This approach works well during the spring but can also be effective in the wintertime if you use a midge or small Pheasant Tail for the dropper.

You'll also encounter places where the river is shallower near the middle but deeper along the banks. In other words, these are stretches made

Amanda Hoppers drifts a nymph through a promising run on the Toccoa DH water.

up of two big runs (one along each bank) with a shallower area in between. The midstream shallow zone may allow anglers to wade along the middle while fishing the deeper water on both sides. These are definitely worth some attention. The trick is to get across the deep runs to the shallow midsection; floating anglers may have an edge in that department.

Yet another type of water that's fairly common here is what one Toccoa regular calls "the deeps" – that is, areas of great depth. They sometimes hold large fish. One of the best known is the deep hole located near the water level gauge on Old Dial Road. Another is the long, deep stretch that you'll find not far upstream from the end of the DH water. In that particular area, also note the streamside vegetation along the outside of that bend. This is a good area to cast a streamer as close to that cover as you dare. In fact, that technique will prove effective anywhere on the river where deep water and streamside cover are found together.

One-hundred-percent catch and release regulations help make the Toccoa Delayed Harvest section a great north Georgia fishery.

Part 4: The Tailwater

Blue Ridge Dam to McCaysville City Park

- How we got the tailwater
- A tailwater overview map
- Wade or float?
- Understanding water releases
- Fishability at different flows
- Toccoa tailwater safety
- Tips for tailwater first-timers
- Section 1: Dam to Tammen Park
- Section 2: Tammen Park to Curtis Switch
- Section 3: Curtis Switch to Horseshoe Bend Park
- Section 4: Horseshoe Bend Park to Toccoa River Park

Toccoa tailwater

Before we jump into the specifics, here's an overview of the Toccoa River tailwater.

Tailwaters are, by definition, stretches of river located directly below dams. Their flow and level are determined primarily by the amount of water being released from the dam, and the released water is often cold...which makes it ideal for trout!

The Toccoa tailwater begins at the foot of Blue Ridge Dam, a 175-foot-high, 1,553-foot-long earth dam which forms Lake Blue Ridge. Construction of the dam began in 1925 and was finished in 1931. The dam was at that time the largest earth dam in the southeast. It is now owned and operated by the Tennessee Valley Authority, and its powerhouse includes a single main generator with a capacity of 13 megawatts.

Today, the tailwater is a nationally-known trout fishery. Its popularity has grown steadily, fueled in part by continued tales of large fish.

But hard times hit the tailwater in 2010 when needed repairs to the dam caused large quantities of warm water to be released into the river. Combined with a hot summer that year, that severely impacted the tailwater fishery. For a time conditions were bleak. However, thanks to the

The Toccoa tailwater begins at the foot of Blue Ridge Dam and continues downriver for more than 14 miles.

efforts of the Georgia Department of Natural Resource, the U.S. Fish and Wildlife Service, TVA, Trout Unlimited, and others, the Toccoa tailwater has rebounded dramatically and is again growing big fish. Several trout approaching 10 pounds have turned up in recently surveys – as did an enormous 15-lb. brown which was measured and then returned to the river in the fall of 2014.

"There are some monster browns swimming around in the tailwater right now," says John Damer, fisheries biologist with Georgia DNR.

Today, the Toccoa tailwater is definitely back on the "A" list. Improvements to the dam have helped the tailwater, too, among them a small supplemental turbine which now maintains a minimum flow of water in the river downstream from the dam.

Photo courtesy Georgia Department of Natural Resources

Georgia DNR fisheries biologist John Damer with a 15-lb. brown trout sampled from the tailwater during the fall of 2014. The fish was returned to the river... and is presumably still there!

Additionally, an oxygenation system boosts the dissolved oxygen content of released water. The bottom line: for the Toccoa tailwater, the future looks bright indeed.

Wade or float?

The tailwater offers plenty of flexibility in terms of how you approach it. Portions of the tailwater are wadable, and all of it is floatable (if the water level is right and if you have the right kind of boat).

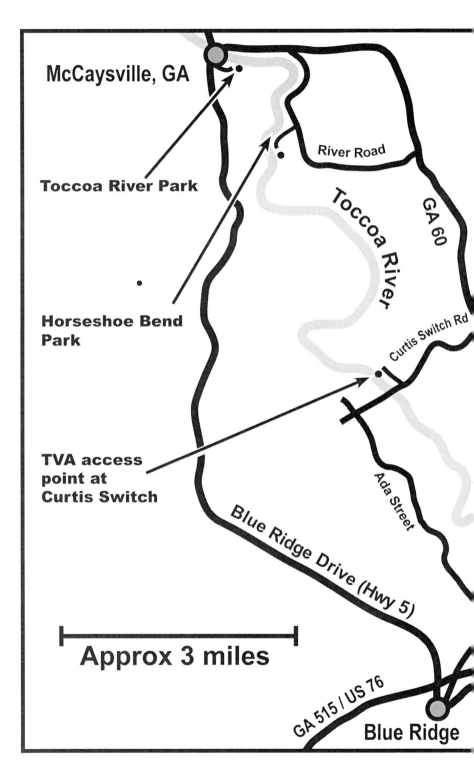

Toccoa Tailwater Overview

Blue Ridge Dam to Toccoa River Park

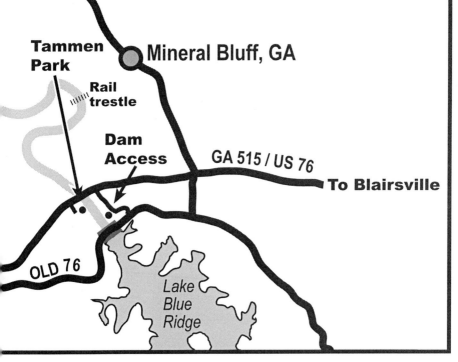

Wading anglers will find potential wad-fishing areas in the vicinity of each of the Toccoa's five public access points (the dam, Tammen Park, the parking area near Curtis Switch, Horseshoe Bend Park, and Toccoa River Park). Although much of the tailwater is bordered by private property, wading is generally okay as long as you don't go beyond the high-water line. Beyond the high-water line you're almost certainly trespassing on private property.

Those who know the Toccoa well agree that wade-fishing in the Toccoa can be an effective way to fish. It lets you proceed at exactly the pace you choose, and it gives you a great deal of flexibility in terms of how you approach and cover the water.

But as much fun as wading can be, at best it gives the fly fisher access to only a limited portion of the tailwater. That's because this river includes many long and deep sections that are simply too deep to wade through – and once you come upon one of them, the wading must necessarily come to an end.

To deal with that challenge, Toccoa veterans have learned that the way to get the most from this tailwater is to fish it while floating the river in a drift boat or similar craft. Of course, you'll need the right kind of boat – that is, one with oars (which will allow you to move you through the deep, slow sections) and also one that doesn't draw too much water (so you'll also be able to get you through the very shallow stretches that you'll encounter too). Otherwise, you may find yourself doing a lot of very slow drifting and even slower dragging. In fact, if you don't have the right kind of boat, your downriver progress can become so slow that you may run out of daylight long before you run out of river and reach your takeout!

You should only float the Toccoa if you have the necessary skills and the right gear. If you have any doubts about your boat's capabilities or about your own ability to handle this river, you're better off wading or arranging a float trip with a guide.

Understanding water releases

To effectively (and safely) fish the Toccoa tailwater, you must understand how water releases at Blue Ridge Dam can impact the river and thus affect your trip.

The water level in the tailwater is affected by several things, including such natural factors as the amount and intensity of rain in the watershed. But the biggest factor impacting the tailwater's flow is always going to be the amount of water released through Blue Ridge Dam. If you are

Toccoa guide Becky Hulsey (wife of Toccoa guide David Hulsey) with a nice Toccoa rainbow. For many fly fishers, especially those with limited time, a guided float trip may be the best way to experience the tailwater.

Photo by David Hulsey

fishing below the dam, you need to understand releases and release schedules. They will have a direct and potentially dramatic impact on your fishing.

Most of the water flowing in the Toccoa tailwater must first pass through Blue Ridge Dam. The powerhouse at the dam generates electric power using a single primary turbine, and water flowing through that turbine is the major contributor to flow in the tailwater downstream. In other words, when that turbine is running, the river below the dam will be high.

There's also a much smaller secondary turbine and generator which runs constantly. This smaller turbine was installed to provide a constant minimum flow. That's *very* good news for the fishing community since it keeps a small amount of water flowing at all times. That's especially important during the summertime, when river temperatures might otherwise get too high for trout.

To recap: If only the small turbine is running, then the river will be low. If the main turbine is running, then the river will be high. In other words, the flow in the Toccoa tailwater is either "on" or "off" depending on whether or not that main turbine is running.

Even though we as fly fishers would like to think that the sole purpose of Blue Ridge Dam is to provide us with a great tailwater fishery, that's not the case. Much though we hate to admit it, fishing considerations are not what drives the operation of the dam.

But knowing how tailwater flow changes at various times and places will go a long way toward making your Toccoa outings fun, successful and safe. That's what we'll focus on next: understanding tie impact of water releases from Blue Ridge Dam.

The first step: Figuring out the Blue Ridge Dam release schedule
When does the main turbine run? That's the big question. Generation schedules vary from day to day, and periods of generation can be as short as an hour or two or can continue around the clock.

That's why you should start every trip by finding out the expected "when" and "for how long" of the day's water releases. There are several ways to get this info. One is via phone at (800) 238-2264, where a series of menus lets you access the predicted Blue Ridge Dam release schedule:

- **Press "4"** to access info on "predicted units" (that is, how many generators will be active. In the case of Blue Ridge Dam, that will be either one or none). Then...
- **Press "23"** to listen to the predicted generating (release) schedule for Blue Ridge Dam.

To summarize, here's how to get water release data for Blue Ridge Dam via phone:

Dial (800) 238-2264, press "4" and then press "23"

You can also access predicted release information online. To access this online data, visit the following site:

www.tva.gov/lakes/brh_r.htm

Next-day release info tends to be most accurate after about 5:30 p.m. *But remember this*: release predictions are *tentative and subject to change*. Unexpected releases *can and do* occur in response to increased power demand, equipment failure, and lake level management needs, among other things. Always plan for unexpected rising water, and always be prepared with an exit strategy that'll get you off the river *fast*.

The next step: Understanding how water levels affect river access
To see how the generation schedule can impact your fishing plans for the Toccoa tailwater, let's take a look at an example.

Say you have just a few hours and want to fish the short stretch between the put-in at Blue Ridge Dam and Tammen Park just downstream. Specifically, let's assume that you want to fish on a Sunday afternoon between 4 p.m. and 6 p.m.

You check the schedule and learn that it calls for "no generators" during those hours. That means that only the small turbine will be running, so only the minimum flow (generally about 145 cfs) will be in the river. At that minimum flow, the level of the river below the dam is about

1540.75 feet. That's ideal for wading, so your Sunday trip looks good.

Now let's say that you decide to stay over and fish the next morning (Monday) from 9 a.m. till 11 a.m. How will the tailwater be then?

To find out, you again start by checking the water release schedule. Let's say that you learn that "one generator" is scheduled to be active from 9 a.m. till 3 p.m. Monday morning. That means that the flow will skyrocket to about 1550 cfs and the river below the dam will rise about 2.5 feet. The quiet and gentle flow of Sunday afternoon will then be high, fast, and unwadable. It's good that you fished on Sunday, because Monday morning isn't looking too good!

The final step: Using release data to plan your fishing

So what can you do if you encounter such a situation? Should you give it up and head for home?

Maybe not.

Before packing it in, think about whether there are alternate places on the tailwater where you *could* fish safely. The rising water obviously doesn't appear everywhere at once but instead moves downriver at a rate of about three miles per hour. The farther from the dam you are, the longer it takes for released water to have an impact. That makes it possible to leapfrog high water and fish downstream areas *before the rising water gets far enough downstream to affect them.*

Though it can be a little unnerving to fish in a river while knowing that there's a pulse of high water bearing down on you from somewhere upstream, this can be a practical way to approach tailwater fishing on the Toccoa. It works because there's always a lag between a release at the dam and the subsequent appearance of released water at any given point downriver – and the farther downriver you go, the longer that lag time will be.

High-water fishing from the bank?

Is it possible to fly fish from the bank during high water? Maybe.

Your first challenge will be the matter of finding a place from which to cast. Water access via the bank is very limited along most of the Toccoa tailwater, as much of the tailwater riverbank is private land. You'll be limited to public access areas.

Secondly, remember that the banks along the tailwater may not be stable. In some areas, the bank will be undercut or soft. You don't want the ground to give way under your feet and dump you into the river.

Approximate times for released water to get from Blue Ridge Dam to...

Location	Approximate river distance below Blue Ridge Dam (total)	Approximate time for water to get there from Blue Ridge Dam*
Tammen Park	A few hundred yards	A few minutes
Curtis Switch	About 7.2 miles	About 2 hours 15 minutes
Horseshoe Bend	About 13.2 miles	About 4 hours 25 minutes
Toccoa River Park	About 14.3 miles	About 4 hours 45 minutes

For safety's sake, give yourself an ample safety margin!

> **IMPORTANT!** These times are NOT float times! Instead, they indicate approximately how long it takes until the river starts to rise following a water release from the dam. Plan to be OFF THE WATER before the time is up. Do NOT stay to make even "one more cast," or you may find yourself caught in dangerous and fast-rising water!

The table at the top of this page shows *approximate* lag times between the start of a release at the dam and the arrival of that released water at several downstream points. Note that they are *not* float times but are instead the *approximate* amount of time it takes rising water to reach various downstream locations.

Here's how you might use the info in that table to turn your day into a good one. Even though the water release predictions suggest that you won't be able to fish between the dam and Tammen Park during your 9-11 a.m. window, you should be able to safely access and fish the river (unless other factors such as rain have made the water come up) if you simply go some distance downriver.

For example: From the table, you learn that it takes about 2 hours for rising water to show up at Curtis Switch, located a bit more than 7 miles downriver from the dam. That means that about 2 hours after the release from the dam, the water near Curtis Switch will begin to rise. Putting it another way, the river at Curtis Switch should remain low until the pulse of rising water begins to arrive about 11 a.m. or so.

Of course, you could go even further downstream and have even longer to fish. For example: at the Horseshoe Bend access, located about 13.2 miles below the dam, you'd have just over four hours before the rising water begins to become a factor.

Fishability at different flows

The Toccoa tailwater is constantly changing. You may encounter the river during no generation, during full generation, or during times of transition from one to the other. You may also see it when it's been impacted by rains in the watershed. It's almost like a bunch of different rivers rolled into one.

Do those different phases fish differently from one another? Indeed they do. In fact, that's the next piece of the Toccoa tailwater puzzle – figuring out how to fish what sometimes seems to be an ever-changing river.

During a release: When water is being released from Blue Ridge Dam, the tailwater is a wild, fast, and turbulent flow. But is it fishable? For wading an-

---

What about a high-water float?

Let me say right up front that I'm with those who do *not* recommend trying to float the Toccoa tailwater during high water. Even many of the guides who make a living on the river are hesitant to float the tailwater a high water.

This kind of floating calls for lots of river knowledge plus a high degree of fast- and rough-water water boat handling skill – not to mention a boat that's up to the challenge. And don't forget that the boat must be a drift boat or a raft with a rowing frame.

Also, be aware of hazards on the river. These include the railroad trestle about two miles below the dam between Tammen Park and Curtis Switch. This trestle, located near Hogback Road, can be a deadly obstacle. Passages through it may be blocked by logjams or debris, making it extremely dangerous. Pre-float scouting is essential, and you should not hesitate to pull the plug on your trip if this obstacle appears impassable.

Remember that *you* are the one responsible for your safety on the river – not me, not the TVA, not the guy at the gas station who said to go ahead and try it.

At any water level, do not attempt a float unless you're sure your skills are up to the task. *You must be brutally honest about your abilities.* If in doubt, don't!

> **You should never try a high-water tailwater float in a float tube!**

glers, of course, fishing during high water is completely out of the question. If you're a wader and they're releasing water at Blue Ridge Dam, forget it. Wait for the water to recede or go fish one of the other streams in the area instead.

What about *floating* in a drift boat or raft during a water release?

"Once the water clears following the initial surge of a release," notes Toccoa guide David Hulsey, "baitfish hang out right on the edge of the flow, tight against the shore." Those baitfish are seeking calmer water close to the bank. Trout, too, like to get out of the current by hugging the edges, and that opens up an interesting opportunity for the angler who can throw a nice, fat streamer up against the bank. You may not catch a lot of fish this way, but the ones you do catch may be memorable.

For this kind of fishing, go with meaty-looking patterns such as the Sculpzilla. Fish them on an intermediate or sink-tip line using a fairly short and relatively heavy leader.

You've got to be fast to fish the tailwater during high flows. There's no slowing down to plan your presentations, and you won't have much time to execute each cast. You need precision, too, because your target zone along the edge is just inches wide.

The whole process has been described as kind of like trying to thread a needle while driving fast on a bumpy road!

If you misjudge a cast and your fly hangs up in streamside limbs, you

A solitary fly fisher explores the tailwater at Horseshoe Bend Park during low water (no generation). That's an ideal time for wading at several tailwater access points, and fishing can be good – especially right after the water comes down following the end of a release.

just kiss that fly goodbye.

"There's no back-rowing to retrieve a fly," David says. Instead, you chalk it up, break it off, tie on another...and cast again.

These complexities (and the challenges of high and potentially dangerous water) make high-water fishing on the Toccoa tailwater an endeavor that's not for beginners.

"Very few want to try it at high water," David says. Because it's so risky, he adds, many guides (including himself) generally do not do guided trips on the tailwater under high-water conditions.

During falling water: Once the water release ends and the river level starts to drop, things change on the Toccoa tailwater. In fact, that period of time immediately following the end of a release is a favorite time for many Toccoa tailwater anglers.

How you approach this window of opportunity depends on whether you're floating or wading.

If you're in a boat or raft, you may be able to time your float so you ride along near the back edge of the falling water. This can provide an extended period of falling-water fishing if you work it just right.

If you are wading, you may be able to prolong the fun by fishing behind the falling water in one area, then jumping in the ol' pickup truck to leapfrog down the river to fish behind that same stage of falling water in another area. Many wading Toccoa anglers view such leapfrogging as an essential tailwater skill, and because road access is generally good this is entirely feasible to do.

Interestingly, falling water on this tailwater seems to have an impact on insect activity in the river. Apparently there is something about the drop in water level that triggers hatches. Exactly what sort of hatch might be triggered on any given day will depend on a number of factors, including the section of river you're fishing as well as the time of year, but it's not unusual to see blue-winged olives and midges coming off as the water falls. It can be a good time to try your luck with a dry fly or a dry-and-emerger combination. And even if you don't see surface activity, don't hesitate to try subsurface offerings such as nymphs or emergers to imitate the underwater insect forms that are almost certainly active...no matter what's visible up above.

Low-water fishing: Most fishing on the Toccoa tailwater is done during periods of low water (that is, when there's no water release from Blue Ridge Dam). If you're floating, low water means that you'll enjoy a much less harrowing run without having to worry about handling a boat, raft, or pontoon in heavy flow. And if you're wading? Then low water means that *much* more of the river will be accessible to you. The upper tailwater between the dam and Tammen Park, some shallow sections in the Curtis Switch area, and the extensive run of river at Horseshoe Bend all open up to the wading angler at low water. At such times, a wading angler can move around the river and access a lot of great water – and more water to fish usually means more fish to hand.

During low water, fish may tend to concentrate in deeper holding areas. Thus, you'll want to thoroughly fish deeper runs. Try nymphs or emergers, either near the surface or with weight to get them down.

This can be a good time for topwater action, too, so always carry a selection of seasonally appropriate dry flies. Many also like to use attractor patterns such as Stimulators or Wulff patterns.

And by all means spend some time trying a dry-and-dropper combo.

What happens when the tailwater comes up?

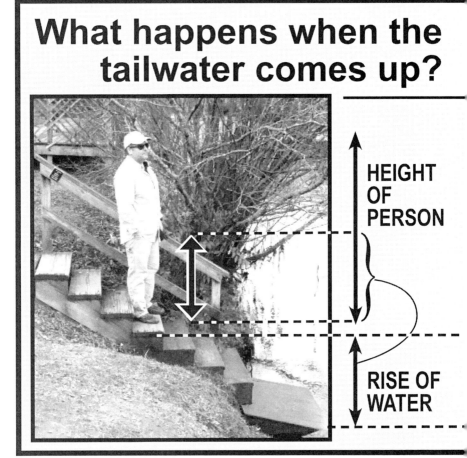

"Often, when there's no generation, it's a good time to try a dry and dropper," guide David Hulsey says. A high-floating dry fly paired with a small nymph or emerger can be exceptionally effective. If you're not sure what to use for a dropper, always remember that a suitably sized soft-hackle Pheasant Tail is often hard to beat.

Finally, if there's been a recent stocking in the area you're fishing, be sure to try patterns such as the Y2K, Sucker Spawn, Yarn Egg and San Juan Worm. Fish these just as you would a nymph.

And, as we said in the section on Toccoa River flies, don't forget to try some streamers. They'll often draw strikes no matter what else is happening on the water.

Does the action slow once the water is low? Some feel that it does, especially near the dam. Why might that be? We'll have to ask the trout

Here are two photos that give you an idea of how the water level in the tailwater can change from "no generation" (that is, minimum flow) to "generation" (that is, when there's a release. These pictures were made one morning at Tammen  Park not far below Blue Ridge Dam. Time between the photos is less than 15 minutes.

During that brief interval, the water level changed in the Toccoa tailwater by almost three feet – and that's three feet of very cold and very fast water.

Here's the "fifty-under-a-rock" technique...just one of many ways to keep yourself aware of the river!!

to know for sure, but here's one possible explanation. During the heavy flow of a release, the trout tend to hunker down somewhere out of the current. Later on, as the water level begins to drop, that current slows and the fish don't have to expend so much energy to move around. They become more active, grabbing those tasty morsels that the high flow dislodged or whatever insects the falling water might have triggered into hatching. But then once the high water has moved on and the flow has settled back to its minimum, it's almost like the fish may say, *"Well, that was fun... but now we're done for a while. Let's take a break till the next round!"*

If you're near the dam:
Listen for the siren, watch for the lights

Blue Ridge Dam now has a siren and light system (installed in 2012) to warn river users of impending releases. This siren is audible between the dam and Tammen Park, a section popular with wading anglers.

The siren usually sounds just prior to a water release, and *if you hear it you should leave the river immediately.*

Does the siren *always* sound prior to water release? That's the hope, but you do not want to bet your life on that! Water releases can occur for a variety of reasons and without warning. Always be alert.

Toccoa tailwater safety

Okay, it's time for "the talk" – the tailwater safety talk, that is.

Why do we need to talk about safety? Because this tailwater can be a dangerous place to fish if you're not attuned to the impact of water releases from Blue Ridge Dam.

The big key to Toccoa tailwater safety is to stay off the river when it's high. That applies whether you're wading or floating. Waders can literally be swept away by high water, while floaters must deal with fast, turbulent flows and some potentially dangerous obstructions.

The first step, as noted earlier, is to *check the predicted release schedule.* Recall that you can do that by calling (800) 238-2264 then pressing "4" and "23."

You can also access predicted release information online by visiting **www.tva.gov/lakes/brh_r.htm**. While not set in stone, the info you will

---

Dealing with the unthinkable

Caught in a release!

Every year, somewhere in the country, unfortunate anglers get caught in rising water. It can happen to anyone. The water comes up without warning, or it takes longer to get to shore than you thought it would, or you decide to make that fateful "one more cast" but then run out of time.

In each of those cases, you could find yourself swept off your feet and carried downriver.

Should that happen on this or any tailwater, experts agree that there are things you can do to increase your odds of survival. Here are some suggestions, including several from the TVA:

First, stay calm. That's easy to say, but it's critical in a crisis situation such as this.

Second, immediately drop everything you're carrying. Yes, even your rod. You've got other more important things to worry about – notably your life – and you don't want to be distracted by worrying about an item of fishing tackle.

Try to float on your back, feet up and pointed downstream. That helps you deal with rocks while reducing the risk of getting your feet trapped.

Do not try to swim upstream. You will exhaust yourself. Instead, try to swim diagonally toward the nearest shore.

Do not try to stand up until and unless you reach a shallow area of slow current.

If you should crawl from the river only to find yourself marooned on an island or on a rock, don't try to swim from there to the main river shore. Instead, stay where you are and call or signal for help. Experienced tailwater anglers carry a small whistle in a pocket against just such an eventuality; they know that the shrill blast of the whistle would be easy for rescuers to hear.

find is generally indicative of what you can expect and when you can expect it.

But even with careful planning, surprises (such as unexpected releases) may come along. Release schedules can and do change – and if you're in the river, you *must* be aware of that possibility.

What can you do to make sure you're prepared just in case?

One way to stay safe on any tailwater is to always be alert for changes in the river. Experienced tailwater anglers are constantly aware of the river around them. How does it sound? How does it feel? They know that the river itself can give clues that an unexpected release is bearing down on you.

How do you attune yourself to a river? Simply look and listen for any changes that might indicate that the water is beginning to rise.

For example, pick out a partially submerged rock, noting the water level. Glance at that rock periodically. If what you see suggests that the water is coming up, exit the river immediately. Don't make "a few more casts" but head for shore right away.

Also note the sound and feel of the river. If you detect any change in the sound of nearby shoals or rapids, exit the water right away. Do the same if you feel any difference in flow against your legs. Resist the temptation to stick around and see if the changes you perceive are real. Instead, err on the side of caution and don't take a chance. Head for land.

One angler I know says that when wading the Toccoa, he will take a $50 bill and place it under a rock near the water's edge.

"I don't want to lose fifty bucks," he says, "so if I think the water's coming up I get out of the river fast to recover the cash!"

Now I don't know if that story is true or if he's just using it to underscore an illustration, but his point is well taken!

To summarize, remember that staying aware is a key to tailwater safety. Remember these four indicators:
- A shift in the sound of nearby rapids or shoals.
- A change in water clarity.
- An increase in the amount of leaves, twigs or debris in the water.
- In-river rocks or logs that unexpectedly disappear from view.

Any of these is a clear signal to get out of the water *right now*.

There are several additional considerations that can help you stay safe on the Toccoa tailwater. Here's what the experts suggest:

Wear a life preserver (PFD): Smart tailwater anglers *always wear a personal floatation device (PFD)*. It will help to keep you afloat should you find yourself unexpectedly in the water. PFDs designed for anglers won't interfere with mobility or with casting, yet they provide the floatation you need. Some of them even resemble suspenders and can be quickly inflated if needed. There are many options that will do the job.

Use a wading belt: One often overlooked wading accessory is a simple wading belt. Fastened around your waist outside your waders, it can help keep water out of your waders should you take an unexpected spill. Chest waders usually come with wading belts, and you should make it a habit to use that belt when wading – especially on a tailwater such as the Toccoa.

Special boating considerations

As we've noted, some stretches of the tailwater are easily wadable. But much of it is better suited for fishing from a drift boat or raft – and if you're boating on a tailwater, there are some special considerations to keep in mind.

First, be aware that the water can be fast and rough during a release. Torturous currents create tremendous turbulence that can swamp small boats in an instant – especially close to the dam.

Don't believe it? Then check out a video on the TVA website (**tva.gov/river/hazwater/index.htm**) which shows what happens when small boats and dam-release turbulence mix. This chilling little snippet is barely 90 seconds long, but it'll give you a whole new appreciation for the power of released water near a dam.

Here are more tips from TVA for safe boating on a tailwater:

- *Always wear your life jacket (PFD).*
- *Never anchor below the dam.* Suddenly rising water could cause the anchored end of the boat to dip and take on water before you can free the boat.
- *Leave the motor running if you're in a powered boat.* In an emergency, you don't want to waste time trying to start the motor.
- *No matter how tempting they look, stay out of restricted areas.* They're marked off for a reason!

If you don't have a wading belt, pick one up at your local fly shop.

Use a wading staff: This simple accessory can greatly enhance your stability when wading – and it can thus be a lifesaver if you need to move quickly (for example, to get off the river in the face of rising water).

Fish with a buddy: Although many anglers (including myself) sometimes enjoy fishing alone, it's always better to fish a tailwater with a buddy. Having a buddy along greatly increases the chances of detecting changing conditions. Two sets of eyes and ears really are better than one when it comes to picking up signs of rising water, and you can also remind each other when it's time to leave ahead of an anticipated release.

Tips for Toccoa tailwater first-timers

James Bradley of Reel 'em In Guide Service has fished the Toccoa tailwater for many years. He's helped thousands of fly fishers discover how much fun the Toccoa tailwater can be, and here he shares several tips that will help any first-timer get more out the Toccoa tailwater adventure.

Be observant: James' first word of advice is to keep an eye on the river's level...because on the Toccoa water releases don't always come when they're supposed to. Pick out a rock or log and keep an eye on it, he says. "If you think you see the water beginning to rise at all," he adds, "get out of the river right away!"

Expect cold water: The Toccoa tailwater can get cold. Water coming out of Blue Ridge Lake is in the low 50s all year long, and James underlines the importance of dressing accordingly. He recommends wool socks and fleece layered with guide pants. Above the waist, he adds, layer appropriately for the season.

Fish in lanes: "For anglers used to small streams," James says, "one of the hardest things is that the tailwater is so large." He suggests approaching your fishing in lanes, working your way across the river and repositioning each cast 1 or 2 feet as you go. "Cover the width of the river, then move upstream and repeat the process," he says. "Otherwise you may miss fish out in the middle of the river because you never put a fly in front of them."

Match the size of the bugs you see: When targeting rising fish, he says, "Always be prepared to match the size of what you see as closely as possible." Size is the most important factor. Later, as the hatch fades and you add a dropper or switch to a nymph, try to pinpoint whether you're seeing mayflies or caddisflies so you'll know what sort of nymph to tie on.

Embrace streamers: Speaking of flies, James notes that fly fishers on the tailwater should be open to using streamers. "Streamers are something you should not turn away from," he says, and he has stories of how a switch to streamers was all it took to save the day. In fact, he adds, a good streamer-style strip retrieve can be a useful technique for any Toccoa tailwater fly fisher.

Here's a look at the entire upper section (Section 1) of the Toccoa tailwater as seen from the GA 515 bridge. At low water, it is possible to wade this entire stretch.

Tailwater section 1:
Dam to Tammen Park

The uppermost section of the Toccoa tailwater is the short stretch from Blue Ridge Dam downriver to Tammen Park near US 76/GA 515. It's very popular with fly fishers, thanks to good wading, easy access, and plenty of fish.

Accessing this section of the tailwater

You can access this section at two points. The first is near the foot of the dam, on river right, where you'll find a small parking area with rock riprap and a set of steps leading to the river. This access point puts you on some very good wading and is also a great starting point for a quick float tube run down to Tammen Park (the second access point, located just downriver). Though there's no ramp, it's also possible to launch a small boat or raft at the dam. In fact, since there's no ramp at Tammen Park, the access point at the dam is usually the starting point for longer floats down to Curtis Switch.

The second access point on this section is at Tammen Park, a developed recreation area about 0.6 mile downstream from the dam. Tammen Park includes a ball field, restrooms, benchs, and plenty of parking. It's a

A small parking area just below the dam provides access for anglers who want to float from the dam down to Tammen Park.

popular jumping-in spot for wading anglers, and when the river is low it's possible to wade downriver (at least as far at the GA 515 bridge) and also upriver to the upper access point and parking area near the foot of the dam.

Before we look at fishing in this area, it's worth reminding you one more time of the

Here's Tammen Park at the lower end of the first section of the Toccoa tailwater. There's no boat launching ramp at Tammen Park, but you'll find a set of steps (which are often slippery) leading down to the river.

importance of safety on this tailwater – especially this close to the dam where the effects of a water release are almost immediately felt.

There's a siren at the dam which should give warning of an impending release. If you hear it, exit the river *right now*. But don't depend totally on the siren – or, for that matter, on published release times. Unscheduled releases can always occur. If you even suspect that the water is beginning to rise, head for shore immediately.

Fishing strategies

A variety of flies will work on this section of the tailwater; the bug chart (pp. 20-21) will help you decide what flies to try at various times of the year. But here's an inside tip: experienced fly fishers on this section often start with a midge. Small midge pupae or midge emergers can work very well. Favorite flies include Rainbow Warriors, WD40s, Zebra Midges (red or black), and Copper Johns. Use weight to get them down deep; alter-

Getting there

As shown on the detail map below, both Tammen Park and the parking area at the dam are very easy to access from US 76/GA 515. Tammen Park Road is just west of the 515 bridge over the Toccoa, while N. River Road is just east of that bridge.

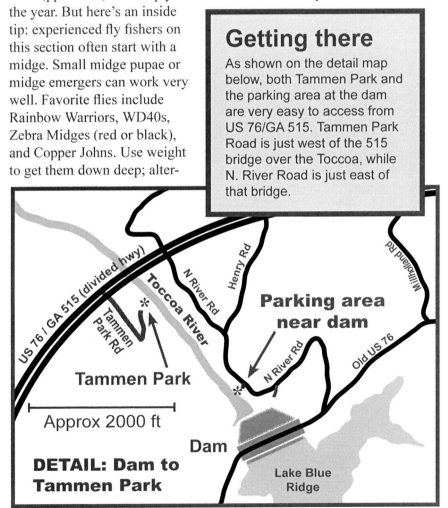

nately, fish them without weight near the surface. In either case, pause at the end of each drift to allow the flies to swing up in the current as if they're dashing for the surface. You can also drop a midge off the back of a dry fly such as an Elk Hair Caddis. Again, use the bug chart to help you choose a suitable dry and suspend the midge about 18 inches below it.

As elsewhere on the tailwater, give streamers a try too. Patterns which suggest a sculpin can be effective and may draw some good strikes when fished along the banks near cover. In fact, that's a good streamer pattern just about anywhere on the tailwater.

Access considerations

With easy access at the dam and Tammen Park, you'll have no problems getting onto this short section of water. Below Tammen Park, however, the next public access is the TVA park at Curtis Switch – another 7.2 miles downriver. Don't miss the takeout or you're in for a long float.

You may see anglers at the dam (as at left) or at Tammen Park waiting for generation to end. They know that once the release ends, the river will drop quickly and some great areas will open up for fishing.

When there's no release, many anglers enjoy exploring the fishable expanses close to the dam.

Tailwater section 2:
Tammen Park to Curtis Switch

The next section of the Toccoa tailwater begins at Tammen Park and continues downstream for about 7.2 river miles to the next public access point at Curtis Switch.

Curtis Switch gets its name from Curtis Switch Bridge, an abandoned bridge built in what bridge designers call the pony truss style. It's one of the few historic iron bridges remaining in this part of the state. In 1983 the old structure was replaced by the modern bridge located just upstream that you see there today, but the remains of the old (and now closed) original bridge still span the river.

In the past, some anglers have parked in the school bus turn-around adjacent to the new bridge, but that's not recommended.

A better parking and access point is the TVA-provided parking area located just a quarter mile further downstream off North Toccoa River Road. You'll find this little riverside park between North Toccoa Road and the river, just before North Toccoa Road becomes gravel. It includes a parking area and a set of steps which lead down the bank and to the water. There is wadable water at here, and it's not ususual to see fly fishers wade fishing in this area.

Here's the old abandoned iron bridge at Curtis Switch, one of only a few such bridges still standing in this part of Georgia.

As you explore this little TVA park, you'll also note a marker there honoring Ted Bogle, Jr., who served as state treasurer of the Georgia Council of Trout Unlimited and who was a founding charter member of

Looking upriver from the TVA Toccoa tailwater access point off N. Toccoa River Road. Water was high when this photo was taken.

the Cohutta Chapter of Trout Unlimited.

What's awaits you along this section of the tailwater? A *lot* of water.

"Some of it is shallow," notes Toccoa guide Jake Darling. By shallow, he says, he means a depth of less than a foot to about 3 feet. On the other hand, there are also stretches that are much deeper. Those deep stretches can slow your drifting to a snail's pace, Jake adds.

That combination of conditions – shallows and deep spots – mean that the best way to float this section is in a shallow-draft craft like a drift boat or a raft...or perhaps even in a pontoon or a kayak. Such craft don't draw much water, allowing you to float through shallow stretches with relative ease. But just as importantly, drift boats or rafts (or pontoons or kayaks) can be paddled through the slow stretches. That keeps you moving downstream, and on a float as long as this one that can be critical if you're to reach your takeout before dark.

"You've got to make sure that you keep moving," Jake says.

Many anglers wonder about fishing this section from a float tube. Is that feasible? No. Why not? Here's one reason: remember that a float tube just drifts along with the flow...and when you're in a float tube, the slow, deep spots can be *really slow.* That can make a trip take much, much longer than you'd think from looking at the route on a map.

The shallows may be just as troublesome because they may be too shallow or easy passage in a float tube. That leaves you no alternative but to walk (not float) 'em while carrying your tube. Believe it: that's an *extremely* slow way to move down a river. Aside from the fact that it eats up fishing time, it can also eat up your daylight and – again – possibly leave you on the river after dark but still some distance from your takeout. You don't want that to happen on any tailwater, especially this one.

That's why there's near-universal agreement that the best way to experience this section of the tailwater (and the next section downstream, too, for that matter) is from the seat of a driftboat or raft. Many outfitters offer guided raft or drift boat trips on the tailwater, and a day spent with one of them can be an exceptionally rewarding way to discover the great fishing on this river. A guide will know the river and its personality and will be familiar with any hazards or tricky spots too. Your guide will also be able to get you tuned in to the fishing with suggestions on where to fish and which flies to use.

Getting there

Float trips from Tammen Park to Curtis Switch will actually begin at the access point directly below Blue Ridge Dam off N. River Road, which turns off US 76/GA 515 just east of the bridge over the Toccoa.

The takeout at the downstream end (the TVA park off N. Toccoa River Road) is accessible from Curtis Switch Road, which turns northwest off GA 60. Takeout access is detailed in the map shown below.

Tackle

When you float the Toccoa tailwater, you'll want to go prepared to match whatever fishing challenges come your way. Use the bug chart on

DETAIL:
Access at Curtis Switch

NOT a recommended parking area!
Even though some park here, it's a better idea to park at the TVA area just downriver.

pages 20-21 to select seasonally appropriate insect imitations. Be sure to add some streamers to the mix. Remember to carry an assortment of egg and worm imitations, too, if there's been a recent stocking.

Because the tailwater varies from shallow to deep, and because different stretches call for different tactics, experienced fly fishers often carry two or three rigged-up rods when floating and fishing this section. One rod might be set up for deep nymphing with weight and a strike indicator, while another might be set up with a dry fly or a dry-and-dropper. A third could be outfitted with an intermediate or sink-tip line and rigged with a streamer. Having multiple rods ready in this way will save you time as you move from one type of water to another by eliminating the need to re-rig every time conditions change.

Access considerations

For those who are wading and who don't have a boat, there's public access to wadable water at Tammen Park and near Curtis Switch.

Those who are floating have limited access options too. Since there's currently no boat ramp at Tammen Park, the only put-in for float trips is at the parking area just upstream from Tammen Park at the foot of Blue Ridge Dam.

The take-out at the end of this section is at the TVA access point just downstream from Curtis Switch Road. There are no other public put-in or take-out facilities on this stretch, and the next public river access is at Horseshoe Bend, about six very long river miles downstream.

Photo by Becky Hulsey

Drift boats are a favorite way to fish much of the Toccoa River tailwater. Here, David Hulsey gets ready for a Toccoa float trip – in a drift boat that he built himself!

Horseshoe Bend Park, at the downriver end of the Curtis Switch to Horseshoe Bend section of the tailwater, offers great wade fishing opportunities.

Tailwater section 3:
Curtis Switch to Horseshoe Bend

The next stretch of this tailwater begins at Curtis Switch and continues downriver for about six river miles to Horseshoe Bend Park. In many ways, this stretch shares characteristics with the Tammen Park to Curtis Switch section just described.

"But there's not as much deep water," notes guide Jake Darling. "There are a lot more shallow stretches and a lot of good dry-and-dropper water."

Because of all those shallow areas, it would be a *seriously* bad idea to try to float this stretch in a float tube...unless you enjoy carrying float tubes down long stretches of shallow sections of river. And believe me: You'd do a lot of that on this section. Carrying a float tube is not nearly as much fun as floating in one!

There's one other difference you'll encounter in this lower section, at least during the warmer times of the year. As you move downstream, the water temperature will tend to rise a bit – especially during the summer. As a result, the quality of the trout fishery may fall off a bit in the sum-

At low water, this V-shaped Native American fish trap is clearly visible in the river just below Horseshoe Bend Park. It's one of several such fish traps still visible along the Toccoa, including several near Horseshoe Bend.

mer in the lower reaches of this stretch due to rising water temperatures.

There's a tradeoff, however. As the water warms, other species become active. You'll still catch some trout, but during the summer it's not unusual to pick up bream or perch now and then. Occasionally you'll even have a bass (maybe even a smallmouth) nail your streamer. It doesn't happen a lot, but it's fun when it does.

Horseshoe Bend Park

For many fly fishers (particularly wading anglers) the highlight of this stretch is Horseshoe Bend Park. Built on land donated by the McCaysville Lions Club, this very nice riverside park marks the downstream end of this section and offers a variety of amenities including picnic tables, walking paths, pavilions, and even live local music at certain times of year. A canoe launch point at the upriver end of the park road provides an easy place to access the water, either to take out a boat (if you've floated down from upriver) or to put in for a short float through the park or a longer float downriver to Toccoa River Park in McCaysville.

The best thing about Horseshoe Bend just may be the fact that it provides direct access to a very long piece of extremely wader-friendly water. In fact, the wading conditions are so good in many areas that you can wade completely across to fish the deeper water on the outside of the bend (assuming of course that the river level is low). This is considered by many Toccoa afficionados to be the easiest wade-fishing you'll find anywhere on the entire Toccoa tailwater.

As you'll discover when you explore here, the bottom features a good bit of gravel. That generally means a good footing. However, there are some slabby rocks that can be very slick. Use extreme care if you find yourself tempted to walk on a large flat rock lest you end up in the water!

You'll also find grass beds through this section. These are worth fishing, particuarly around their margins and especially during spring.

Most fly fishers focus their attention on the outside of the bend where the water is deeper. However, you'll find good runs to work with a nymph or streamer all across

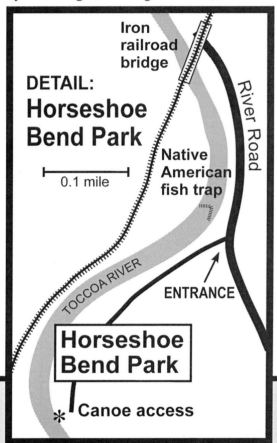

Getting there

To reach Horseshoe Bend Park, follow River Road from GA 60 for about 0.9 miles as shown. You'll pass under an iron railroad bridge. About 0.2 miles beyond the bridge, look for the entry to Horseshoe Bend Park on your right. The entry goes down a hill and then follows the river upstream, passing fishable water all along the way. The canoe access is at the far end of the park road.

What about the upstream end? Reach the upstream end of this section from Curtis Switch Road, which turns west off GA 60.

the width of the river, and you'll also find some great riffle water (for example, opposite the picnic area) that can be a lot of fun with dries or a dry-and-dropper combo. Again, choose flies based on what you see or with the help of the bug chart on pages 20-21.

By the way, today's anglers are not the first to fish in these waters – far from it. The proof is that V-shaped formation of rocks visible in the river from the park entry during low water. It's a fish trap, one of many constructed here by Native Americals long before you or I was even thought of. Knowing that this fish trap is there provides a tangible link to the area's past, and it's not pretty neat to know that you're fishing almost side by side with a shadow of the area's history.

In fact, before you leave, you should be sure to make a few cast with nymphs or streamers around that time-tested V-shaped formation of rocks. Sometimes you'll be rewarded with a nice trout. Then you'll *really* feel that connection with the past.

With lots of water to explore, Horseshoe Bend will become one of your favorite spots on the tailwater. You can easily spend a half day here working your way through this stretch, and when you finish you can always use the other half of the day to go back and fish it all again!

Tackle considerations

When it comes to tackle, considerations on this section of the tailwater are similar to those above Curtis Switch. If you're wading, carry flies to match a variety of seasonal insects; if you're floating, carry two or three rods rigged for different types of fishing in different areas.

During summer, always carry some terrestrials – hoppers, beetles, or ants. Riverside grassy or brushy areas are often loaded with grasshoppers and other terrestrials at that time of year, and it doesn't take a lot of wind to blow some of those hoppers into the water. Trout seem to relish hoppers, so you may do well in such stretches by throwing a big hopper imitation toward the bank and allowing it to drift along.

Access considerations

Whether wading or floating, remember that there are only two public access points along this stretch. The only public put-in for the Curtis-Switch-to-Horseshoe-Bend float is at the TVA park near Curtis Switch, and the only public takeout at the bottom of this section is at the upstream end of Horseshoe Bend Park.

Wading is possible at the Curtis Switch access point and, as we have seen, at Horseshoe Bend Park. But remember that there's no public access in between. The next public access below Horseshoe Bend is at Toccoa River Park in McCaysville.

Tailwater section 4:
Horseshoe Bend to Toccoa River Park

By the time you get to Horseshoe Bend, the Toccoa River tailwater is just about done. The river soon crosses into Tennessee and changes its name to the Ocoee. However, there's still one last section of the Toccoa tailwater to be explored – the short stretch of river from Horseshoe Bend down to Toccoa River Park in McCaysville.

Toccoa River Park is a small developed park located right in the middle of McCaysville, Ga. It features parking, picnic tables, a playground, restroom facilities, a riverside deck and even a paved boat ramp. Near the boat ramp, there's even carved totem pole that's a great landmark.

If you look to the left of the restroom building, you'll see a fish stocking tube. Yes, this is a stocking point. That makes this little park even more appealing to fisherfolk.

The river between Horseshoe Bend and Toccoa River Park has a much more urban feel than does the river above Horseshoe Bend. You'll notice the difference. But the fish don't seem to care if they live in town or in the country, and fishing through here can be good.

This lowermost portion of the tailwater warms faster than the upper stretches, so as you move into the warmer months of the year the water here may not be quite as much to the liking of trout. Rainbow trout will

Toccoa River Park boasts a paved boat ramp – a rarity on the Toccoa tailwater.

tend to move upriver, which may be why some Toccoa regulars talk about this section as one that's good for brown trout.

But there's a tradeoff. The warming water of summer can make this stretch much more comfortable for bass. Now and then, in fact, you may connect with some concrete proof that these river bass like big streamers just as much as do trout.

Wade or float?

Since it's only just over a mile on the river from Horseshoe Bend to Toccoa River Park, this piece of river is sometimes tacked onto the Curtis-Switch-to-Horseshoe-Bend float. However, this run makes a worthwhile short float in its own right. Some Toccoa fly fishers fish this section from float tubes, starting at Horseshoe

Among the things you'll find at Toccoa River Park are a carved totem pole and a fish stocking pipe. Yes, this is a stocking area.

Bend Park and taking out at Toccoa River Park. Having two cars makes such a float a cinch. However, you can do it even with just a single car... if you don't mind the occasional odd look you'll get as you walk through McCaysville and back to the put-in at Horseshoe Bend while toting your float tube! Alternately, if you're a trusting soul, you could leave your tube at Toccoa River Park, hike to Horseshoe Bend, and then drive back to retrieve the tube.

Can you wade in this section? In some places you can. However, you'll find that some areas are much too deep for wading. Thus, to fish the whole stretch, you'll need to float it.

Access considerations

Wading access is straightforward at either the put-in (Horseshoe Bend) or the takeout (Toccoa River Park).

If you're floating, work your way left as you approach the takeout to exit at the paved boat ramp. The totem pole and riverside deck provide good landmarks. Be careful not to miss the takeout.

Getting there

To reach Toccoa River Park from Horseshoe Bend, take GA 60 into McCaysville to Harpertown Road and turn left. Cross the river, then turn left on Market Street. Market Street soon makes a dogleg turn to the left and takes you to the park. There's parking on both sides of the playground/restroom complex. The boat ramp is most easily accessible from the upstream parking area.

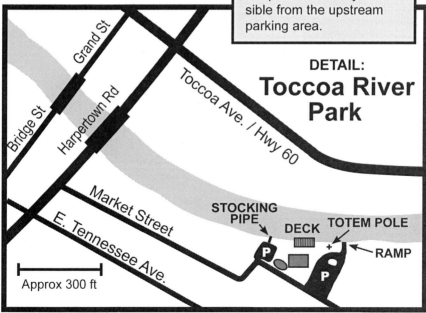

DETAIL: Toccoa River Park

A Toccoa Gallery

"I've got a good one here!"

A personal pontoon gives good access to great water!

Pheasant tail nymphs are a Toccoa favorite!

Photo courtesy Unicoi Outfitters

Waiting at Tammen Park for the water to come down.

Drifting a nymph through a good run.

A nice Toccoa River brown trout.

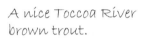

Photo courtesy Unicoi Outfitters

On the Toccoa, the smiles say it all!

Photo courtesy Unicoi Outfitters

Appendix:

Fly shops, guide services and licenses

FLY SHOPS: Several fly shops and guide services serve Toccoa River fly fishers:

Blue Ridge Fly Fishing (fly shop and guide service)
490 East Main Street
Blue Ridge, GA 30513
(706) 258-4080
www.blueridgeflyfishing.com
brflyfishing490@gmail.com

Southern Highroads Outfitters (fly shop and guide service)
253 Hwy 515 E Building 1-C
Blairsville, GA 30512
(706) 781-1414
www.southernhighroadsoutfitters.com
info@southernhighroadsoutfitters.com

Reel'em In Guide Service (guide service)
James Bradley
1890 Burnt Mountain Road
Ellijay, Georgia 30536
(706) 273-0764 or (877) 647-4534
www.reeleminguideservice.com
jbradley@ellijay.com

Unicoi Outfitters (fly shop and guide service)
7280 S. Main Street
Helen, GA 30545
(706) 878-3083
www.unicoioutfitters.com
flyfish@unicoioutfitters.com

LICENSES: The Toccoa is designated as trout water, and you must have the proper fishing and trout licenses to fish there. You should be able to purchase the appropriate licenses online at **http://gofishgeorgia.com/licenses-permits-passes.**